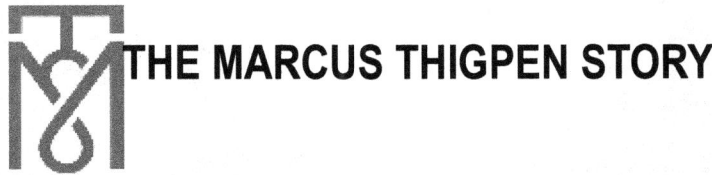 **THE MARCUS THIGPEN STORY**

Copyright © 2018 Marcus Thigpen.

All rights reserved. No part of this book may be used or reproduced by any means, graphic, electronic, or mechanical, including photocopying, recording, taping or by any information storage retrieval system without the written permission of the publisher except in the case of brief quotations embodied in critical articles and reviews.

Printed in the United States of America

ISBN: 978-1-7334325-2-8

CONTENTS

PREGAME ACKNOWLEDGMENTS & DEDICATIONS i

1ST QUARTER THE DISASTER 5
   1 THE COIN TOSS 7
   2 THE KICKOFF 10
   3 FIVE YARD PENALTY 14
   4 FIRST DOWN 21

2ND QUARTER THE DEDICATION 33
   5 SECOND DOWN..35
   6 FALSE START..39
   7 SIDELINE INFRACTION 47
   8 SUBSTITUTION 59
   9 ILLEGAL HIT 70
   10 THIRD DOWN 73
   11 TWO MINUTE WARNING 80
   12 TIME OUT 90

HALFTIME 95

3RD QUARTER THE DREAM 113
   13 ADJUSTMENTS..115
   14 FLAG: DELAY OF GAME...123
   15 EXTRA POINT 131
   16 MOVING THE CHAINS 137
   17 TOUCHDOWN...142
   18 GAME WINNING DRIVE..159

4TH QUARTER THE DRIVE..169
19 BACKED UP 171
20 EJECTED 176
21 A NUMBERS GAME 183

PREGAME

ACKNOWLEDGMENTS & DEDICATIONS

This book is dedicated to the late La'Crecia Daniels, her friends and the Daniels family. You are my inspiration and the reason why I push to be great daily. I made a promise to always do right by you by the way I live my life. I know you're watching over me as my personal guardian angel and I know you would be proud of the man I have becoming.

- My father, the late Marcus Joseph, a great man and amazing person all around.

- The late Tahir St. Clair, who always believed in me and pushed me to higher levels. I'll always hold you close to my heart!

- My amazing children, Diamond Walker, son Marcus Thigpen Jr., daughter Mariya Thigpen, and my youngest daughter Morgyn Thigpen; you all are my motivation to keep going every single day!

- My mother, Karen Joseph, who taught me the best way she could to be a man and to always finish whatever I started.

- My siblings, Kiyette Joseph, Allante Joseph, Travontae Joseph, and Delaney Joseph. Thanks for pushing me to be the best big brother I could possibly be.

- Kaleb Thornhill, Coach Ken Fenton, Coach/Father Cedric Everson, Coach Robert Lynch, Coach Gerald Brown, Coach Jeff Nixon, Coach Wooley, Coach Rudy, Coach Lewis and the late Coach Hep.

- My accountability partners: Lance Bennett, Nick Polk, Scherone Harris, Kevin Jackson, Adrian Battles, Richard Council, Chris Wheeler, Jeremy Kelley, Tim Plair Anteney Plair, Adam and James Logan.

- Special thank-you to Rhonda Moss, Tawanna Wheeler, Terri and Eric Lewis, Mrs. Tounsel, Lisa and Dennis Strange, my late Uncle Bob and Auntie Bonnie, and Vena Mixon.

- A host of special aunts, uncles, and cousins. There are too many to name, but I love you all deeply.

- Robert Sheets: Thanks for taking a chance on a small-time guy who had a dream. You've been a blessing to me in so many ways, and I thank you for it. Without you I don't know where I would be or even if I would have had an NFL career. Thanks for always "keeping it real"—KRSIII.

These people have truly inspired me to be where I am now in life and continue to drive me to be a better man, father, husband, and friend. It's nothing but the grace of God that has allowed me so many great opportunities and experiences in my lifetime thus far. The people listed above were there for me when I was down to the lowest points in my life. As you read my story, I really hope that you will not only be inspired to be a better person but also learn from what I went through and not make the same mistakes that I made or allow your mistakes to define your purpose. It's my heart's desire that, through my shared experiences, you develop the mindset that you will be the best YOU that you can possibly be, no matter what, because anything short of your best isn't worth it. If you persist through the resistance that life throws at you then it's yours for the taking. Be Blessed!!

RESIST & PERSIST

1ST QUARTER

THE DISASTER

1
THE COIN TOSS

When people are walking to the center of the football field at the fifty-yard line, they're usually the leaders of your team going out there to prepare for the coin toss. At that moment, whether the captain chooses heads or tails, there is a 50/50 chance the coin will land on either one. We have that same chance in life; we can do what's right or we can do what's wrong. The fate of our future lies in this toss-up. As simple and as easy as that sounds, temptations, peer pressure, and immature decision making make the simple, easy things turn into the hard, misguided things that often lead to trouble.

***

The rain was pounding so hard against the windows of that old, green '97 Astro van. With the nighttime glare of the streetlights rejecting off the wet residue, it was almost impossible to see where I was going. I tried my best to drive through the rough, pothole-infested streets of Detroit, barely seeing what was before me. I pulled over to let a friend drive because I knew I had no experience driving in those conditions, but I wanted a piece of the action so bad to impress my friends. Luckily, the rain stopped that night, but it left a slippery path ahead of us. I hopped back into the driver's seat, and the adrenaline was pumping as all of my friends in the car yelled, "Go faster Go faster!" In my fourteen-year-old mind, there was no hesitation to give into the pressure to escalate the situation from fun to fearlessness. I mean, we had already stolen the van, and even though the rain made the streets a bit slippery, we knew if we drove fast enough, we could go airborne over the first hump of the maze for a second or two.

The first two trips over the hump were so much fun, I had to do it again. My palms were sweaty, and my heart almost leaped out of my chest as I clenched the steering wheel. Before I could think twice, my foot weighed heavily on the gas pedal as my friends laughed and giggled in the back-seats, anxiously anticipating the car catapulting us through the air. The van accelerated across the wet terrain—a sharp turn was approaching on the maze we were on, and almost suddenly I could hear the laughter quickly turn into screams of panic as I slid off the road going forty miles per hour in a twenty-five-miles-per-hour zone. The van went flying through the woods, skidding through mud and barely missing trees as I dodged as much as I could, whipping the steering wheel from side to side. I pushed and pushed on the brakes but with the rain and lack of traction, I realized I no longer had any control of the car. Finally . . . boom!

Silence, gas, the smell of airbag dust, and shattered glass quickly filled the van. The airbags deployed and made it hard to see through the thickness of the fumes and smoke streaming from the front of the vehicle. I opened my eyes and there was a tree that completely smashed in the front end of the car, but that was nothing compared to what I saw as the smoke cleared.

Sideline Reflections

What do you do when your worst nightmare comes true? How do you survive?

Think back to something you did in your past that causes you great regret and shame. Dig it up; Find it, and you'll start to get close to understanding what young Marcus went through in that moment.

2
THE KICKOFF

Two weeks prior to the accident, I was "the man" at Henry Ford High School on Detroit's west side. I had all the pretty girls, sold drugs here and there to keep a few extra dollars in my pocket to help my mom out, and hung with only the coolest guys at school, including my older cousins, whom, even as a little kid, I always wanted to be like—talk like, play ball like, and have all the chicks like. I was only fourteen. You couldn't tell me a thing. I played football for the Detroit Panthers, a little-league P.A.L. football team I'd played on since the age of nine. I also ran track at the high school I attended. I was becoming everything I thought I wanted to be. I always made the honor roll and was smarter than most of the kids in my class, but sometimes I hid my intelligence just to fit in and maintain my image and status. When my grades slipped, and more and more trouble found its way to my doorstep, my mother sat me down for a heart-to-heart talk. My mother was only sixteen when I was born, and neither she nor my father graduated from high school. She was always tough on me and only wanted to see me be the best me I could be and make it farther than they had. My mother was always against me going to Henry Ford High School because of the bad reputation it had and the people I was hanging around with. After a lot of begging and pleading, I finally convinced her to let me go. But this was one conversation I'll never forget. She said, "Son, just as quickly as you're getting all these girls, friends, and attention, God can take it all away."

In the back of my mind, I was thinking, *We don't even go to church; how does she know what God will do?* I knew nothing about God and wasn't worried about what my mother said He would take from me. We went to church once a year, and that was on Easter, and we were usually decked out in nice suits. I was so caught up in myself, I completely missed the message. So, ignoring what she had to say, I kept on doing me. I had just completed my first level of driver's training, I was excited and was itching to drive.

Two weeks later, I threw on the freshest outfit I could find, laced up my Jays, made sure my waves were on point, and called all of my friends to see who was going to this hotel party a friend was having that night.

My girlfriend (at the time) mother, and my mother were friends. She came by my house to talk to my mom before driving us to the party that night. I had just gotten my driving permit, so I asked my girlfriend mother if I could drive to the party if she sat on the passenger side. She said, "Sure," after her conversation with my mother. I could finally scratch that itch I had to get behind the wheel. My younger sister, my girlfriend, and two other friends, were all at the house, anxious, dressed, and ready to go to the party we had been waiting for all week. But like most women, my mother and my girl mother were talking way too long about what seemed to be nothing. So we all waited impatiently in the van, with me, of course, in the driver's seat. My girlfriend said, "Go ahead, just take the car; my mother won't mind."

I was nervous at that point, asking, "Are you sure?" We all knew her mom was cool, but to take her car was like a different level of cool. I was shaking a bit—terrified of taking the van, but yet I started it up and then took off. The first stop we made was to go pick up La'Crecia, who happened to be my first girlfriend in elementary school. As we got ready to leave La'Crecia's house, her mother told us to be careful and have fun. La'Crecia sat up front with me on the passenger side. We stopped by the hotel party, but it was still early, and no one was really there yet, so we decided to leave and come back. That's when the rain came. Although I had my Level 1 Driving Segment and passed all the classes, I had never driven in the rain before and, on top of it all, it was getting dark outside.

I pulled over to let one of my friends drive; he had a license and was a more experienced driver. We started getting calls from my girl mother, and I know she was nervous and worried about us, but we couldn't answer because we took the van without permission. We decided we were going to deal with the consequences after we had our fun. We went to Belle Isle, a popular spot in downtown Detroit, and there weren't that many people out there because of the rain so we decided to go through this wooded area that was like a maze. At the beginning of it, if you were going fast enough, you would be airborne for a second. My boy drove through it first, and we were all laughing and having fun. The second time through, I wanted to drive. We went back around and switched drivers, and as I was backing up, I hit a pole. A few of us got out to see the damage, which was a little dent in the rear bumper. My sister told me to just let my friend drive, but I said, "No, I got it."

As we went through the maze again, everyone was so in to it that they were all yelling to me, "Go faster, go faster!" So as I sped up and started going through the maze, it was a sharp turn that changed my life and that of everyone in that van that night—forever.

Sideline Reflections

Sometimes in life we don't see the sharp turns until it's too late.

Our lives are made up of a series of decisions and each decision adjusts the direction of our life. Mostly in small, imperceptible ways...but sometimes more significant ramifications occur.

The challenge is this:

It's hard to know, in advance, which decisions will be small and which decisions will turn out to be more significant.

Football players know that if you want to be good at game time, then you need to first be good in practice.

How we make the small decisions when we have time to think and at moments of very low risk, reflect how we will make the big, critical decisions... when we have less time to think.

The cost of choosing the wrong path in the maze of life can turn deadly. Choose wisely.

Which of these most often drives your decisions? Be honest.

- Feeling versus principles?
- Short-term gain vs long-term gain?
- Emotional baggage?
- Past experiences?
- Rational thinking?
- Peer pressure?

3
FIVE YARD PENALTY

As I slid off the road into the grass, fighting my way through the trees, the van just slid out of control, and then it all came to a screeching halt. I hit a tree head on, and all I could remember hearing was eerie silence in the van. The airbags came out, windows were shattered, and smoke was everywhere. After about a minute or so, I heard moaning and groaning of people in pain, but I couldn't tell from whom or what had happened to them. I immediately got out of the van and went around the back of the car to the right rear side door and slid it open. I pulled out everyone I could as fast as I could, not knowing if the van was about to explode from all the smoke.

As I made my way to the passenger side, it felt like my heart stopped, because all I could see was La'Crecia crushed in her seat. The impact was mostly on her side, so the front end of the van smashed into her. As she sat slouched down in the seat, with her seat belt across her motionless body, I could barely see her face because it was covered in blood. Her brain was showing, and bones in her legs were broken as if she tried to brace herself for the impact. I tried to get her out of her seat belt, but she was stuck, still and silent.

I ran as fast as I could to the roadside where we slid off and tried flagging down somebody—anybody who could help. I was able to get someone to stop for us and call the EMS. I came back to check on everyone and found out one of my friends had a broken wrist, there was a deep gash in another friend head, my little sister was in pain, and all were in shock and groaning from the agonizing discomfort we felt. My friend with the gash on his head had a concussion and couldn't remember anything, and there I was, perfectly fine, with maybe a little cut or two from the shattered glass, and I was saying to myself, How is this even possible? Am I in a nightmare?

Those bright red lights came flashing onto the scene and, at that moment, I knew we had to tell them what happened. My girlfriend and I were planning to say that my friend with the concussion and the gash in his head, was the driver and crashed the car. We both were so afraid of what might happen to me, and because he couldn't recall anything that went on that night, it seemed convenient to put it all on him.

We were all rushed to the hospital to make sure we didn't have any more injuries. Not long after arriving, the questions came rolling, but we stuck to the story. At this point they informed us that we all had to call our parents and tell them the horrific news. All kinds of thoughts and emotions were running through my mind, like, What will my momma think? What will she say? I'm about to go jail. I'm about to get beaten. Our parents rushed to the hospital to see what was going on. Once they arrived, I had to make one of the hardest decisions I ever had to make in my young life. Now am I going to tell them the truth, or will I keep lying on my innocent friend? As scared as I was and as hard as it was, I decided to tell the truth; I had to confess to it and take responsibility for what I had done. After all, I knew it would come out eventually.

The doctors made us all take a breathalyzer test for alcohol consumption to see if it may have contributed to the cause of the crash. No one was drinking, smoking, or doing any type of drugs. It was me being immature and not understanding what could happen behind the wheel of a car. Once we got done, we were all able to go home except for my sister, as they found out her pain came from her liver being bruised from the crash. No one knew where they took La'Crecia and if she was okay. Later that night, the police detective informed my mother of the devastating news that La'Crecia had passed away minutes after the crash. When my mom told me the news, it all felt like a dream—more like a nightmare in that moment—and everything stood still, like time had frozen over that traumatizing moment.

I cried all night in pain and disbelief that this happened, and my mom cried with me, holding and trying to calm and console me as much as she could. I couldn't sleep that night or for the next few weeks because I kept having visions and flashbacks of the accident. I saw it all happening over and over again; the night kept replaying in my head. I had a lot of what ifs. What if we'd waited, what if we didn't go through the second time, what if I just let my friend drive, where would we be? It was hard knowing that I was responsible for a life lost and yet nothing happened to me. I felt guilty and wished it had been me and not her. The word started to get out, and news reporters would knock on our door or question and neighbors about the type of person I was and how this could happen. Our house had just caught fire not long before the accident, so we weren't home to be hounded by the reporters. However, our neighbors would call and tell my mom how they would catch them peeking through our windows and taking pictures of the house, like I was some type of criminal.

I was afraid I was going to have to go to jail, but instead I was put on intensive probation all throughout high school, I was required to go to counseling the first year after the accident and couldn't receive my driver license until age twenty-one. Just when I thought things couldn't get any worse, as the days went on, I started receiving death threats from random people to who were close to La'Crecia—threats that I'd better not come back to school because they were going to hurt or even kill me, and I was accused of causing the accident on purpose. It killed me internally to know that people thought this of me. I would never intentionally put anyone's life in danger. People I cared most for were all in that van that night, and I sincerely never meant for any of it to happen. I quickly went from being "the man" to one mistake, one accident taking it all away, including one of my closest friends. All I could hear was my mother's words resonating over and over in my head: "God can take it all away from you."

With the threats coming left and right, I was warned not to show up at her funeral, but there was no way I could stay away. I was there and had to stay surrounded by my family and friends and be on guard just in case anything got out of hand. I just wanted to pay my respects and really couldn't do that under the circumstances like I wanted to because of the threats. I stood in the back while I listened to her eulogy, trying to fight back my river of tears. The hurt and pain that I felt was indescribable, and there was so much I wanted to get up there and say but couldn't.

At the age of fourteen, I had been through more than most people would experience in their whole lifetime. I was in my very first car accident when I was only a few months old. My mom held me tight as the car rolled over going down the highway; I wasn't injured but my aunt had to get fifty staples in her head, and she was the driver. At the age of seven, I was hit by a car as my uncle told me to run across a busy intersection while walking to the corner store.

This was one of the scariest moments of my life. As I flew in the air and fell down on my face. I was knocked unconscious. The EMS came and rushed me to the hospital. I vaguely remember anything at that moment. I remember seeing bright lights coming and going as I was getting wheeled through the hospital, hearing talking and then nothing. I woke up the next day in the hospital and saw my mother and family in the room by my side. I remember seeing tubes and things connected to me and trying to figure out how I got there.

My mother was angry at my uncle for a very long time.

I healed up and was able to leave the hospital. I was misdiagnosed while I was in there as they told me that the kidney damage that I had was severe and I didn't have long to live. I remember days felt so long as we would sit there and cry not knowing when my time would expires. Nothing happened and at my next checkup we found out that I was going to be fine and it was a mistake on their behalf. That was scary to hear the words that we don't know how much longer you have to live at such a young age or any age for that matter.

My life hadn't even really started yet. I was told to stay away from physical activity so my mother was very aware of the things that I were doing and made sure I was safe.

A couple years went by and all I wanted to do was play football after watching my older cousin play. She would not let me play because I was small and because of what the doctors told us. I told her that I wouldn't get hit that hard and I'll run too fast to get caught, besides the doctor said that it was a mistake and I'm good. After a while she finally let me play.

At the age of fourteen, my girlfriend and I decided that we were not ready to be parents and aborted the baby we immaturely made. I grew up in the hood where hardship was a given and the possibility of success was slim. I watched my mother struggle day in and day out to try to provide for all of my siblings and myself. I did what I could to help mother out because I saw her crying daily, trying to figure out how bills were going to get paid, what we were going to eat, wondering how she would get us something for our birthdays and Christmas. The dedication and drive that my mom had, made me really admire her and her strength. She is one of the toughest and strongest people that I know. Then there was the accident that played the biggest part in changing the course of my life and the path of destruction I was on.

My mentality had quickly switched from wanting to be "the man" to now becoming a man. It was already enough stress on my mother with my dad not being involved the way that she would like him to be in our lives, and for me to add on to that stress was just selfish of me. I hated to see her crying every night. So I made up my mind that I would use this fresh start and do things the right way.

Sideline Reflection

Be "the man"… or be A man.

Do you remember being fourteen? Do you remember those teenage hormones raging?

Where every disappointment was devastating and every crush was true love?

How well-equipped would you have been to handle a life-altering disaster?

Many of us are fortunate to have never had a life-altering occurrence, but setbacks are still common to us all. I was forced to make some hard decisions at a really young age but looking back, I'm confident that they all helped me to get to where I am today.

What setbacks did you have in your childhood that still affect you today?

The 5 most memorable childhood and teenage setbacks I ever experienced were:"

1. _____
2. _____
3. _____
4. _____
5. _____

4
FIRST DOWN

Something had to change. There's a saying by Gary W. Goldstein that goes something like this: "All you can change is yourself, but sometimes that changes everything!" I transferred schools that year to get away from the threats and the haunting past and have a new beginning. I wasn't going to allow anything to bring me back down to where I was.

Prior to the accident and how I got into selling drugs was me being a product of my environment and trying to find a quick way to make money for myself and my household. The drugs that we were selling were actually stolen. I would sit there in my basement trying to figure out ways to make money to help my mother because I didn't want any more nights with no heat where we had to sleep under the cover in our coats in the winter, or walk through the house with candles because our lights were shut off. We had many nights where we didn't know where I next meal would come from and when we didn't find food we would just go to sleep, because if you slept you wouldn't have to think about it.

My brother, my cousin and myself knew a drug dealer in the hood and knew where he kept his product. We made a plan to go in and take his whole stash when he left. We staked out for a while to see what his routine was and when we caught on to it we made our move. We stole what had to be about 10lbs of marijuana and for us at 14 was a lot.

We didn't want people to know that we were selling so we tried to be as discreet as possible trying to figure out how to get it all off. We kept it hidden in the back of a broken down garage until we figured out how to get it off. We asked around and found a buyer after a while. We didn't break it down to sell little bags, we were trying to sell them by the pound. Once we found someone that would buy them from us we started making sales. We were making money that we had never made or even seen before and we knew we had to be smart about it. We would meet often and talk about how to spend it and not be too flashy to turn people eyes toward us.

Fortunately, we were smart enough to buy a few things here and there and though there was a little suspicion, no one really thought anything of it because I had two jobs and my brother and cousin stayed low key with their things.

We were able to get all that we had off and after that we were done with it. We never got into any trouble, nor did we get caught. We were really sneaky and smart with it. You would have thought we had experience the way that we moved. Watching family members and movies we tried learning from their mistakes and though it wasn't a lot where we were making millions, we were still making a ton of money at 14. I was able to help out with bills, food and clothes for my household. Leading up to the accident I was going down this path and this downward spiral kept going.

One day we were going to this girl house to get blowjobs, not knowing that this was a drug house. We went in and seen a few guys there and didn't think anything of it. It was my friend turn to get his blowjob done and when he finished I was next. When he got done, the guys there asked him to pay for his services he received but at that time we didn't have any money because we didn't know what we were getting ourselves into. There were four guys there watching tv smoking weed, and drinking beer. When they found out that we didn't have money to pay them or the girl, they got up and hit my boy in the head with a glass beer bottle and it cracked and the glass cut his neck and they threw us all on the floor and pulled out guns.

I've only heard and seen these type of things on the news and in movies but for this to be happening to me I was distraught. With guns in our face and them yelling I zoned out and started to think of all the things I had done leading up until that point in my life and couldn't believe I was about to die over something so small at such a young age. We were protected and covered that day because one of the guys there recognized my boy. His brother was a big time drug dealer and he knew his older brother and that's what saved us.

He realized that we were just some lost teenage kids. Talk about, who you know or in that case who knew him. They told us to get up, get out and to never come back there. They let us out the front door, and we darted back and forth across the streets as if they were still trying to shoot us.

I had on some new shoes and creased them up bad in the front and was mad about it when I got him. My heart was beating so fast as I was laying across my bed sweating profusely. After what I had just experienced I was worried about how bad I just had messed up my new shoes. That's where my mentality was. All this was going on and no one knew because I kept this façade as if I was the best kid and did no wrong. These were things that led up to my having the accident and at that point when my mother said those words to me, it all started to make sense. I was putting myself in some very crazy situations and would always find myself wondering how I got there.

I left Henry Ford in September 2001 and went to Mumford High School, which ironically was the same school I took my driver's training classes at earlier that year.

On my first day walking into Mumford High School, I was so ready to move on to the next chapter in my life and live right. I had never been so anxious and eager to get back in classes and to meet new friends. No one knew my story, and no one knew what I saw, all I'd done, or any of what I had just gone through, and I wanted to keep it that way as long as possible.

I was afraid that if people knew, I'd be looked at differently and never be given a chance to reach my full potential. I stayed to myself for the first week and did all that was required of me. I went to class, did my work, really didn't talk too much, and went home right after school. I spoke and said hi to people, but that was it. It was eating me up inside to have to watch the track runners and football players play from a spectator's perspective. After asking around school about how to get on the football and track team, I quickly added a football class to my schedule. My first day in my football class, there was a set of twins leading the class when I walked in for the first time. The bigger twin, was the running back, and that was my position; and all I remember thinking was how that was my spot, but in my mind I was thinking there was no way I could get that big. I was always small in size but explosively fast, and that's how I picked up the nickname "Mighty Mouse" growing up. I had too much heart to ever let my size stop me from going after what I wanted, so I set out to take the twin spot. That day I went home and asked my mother for a weight bench, and like most things we asked for, she made it happen somehow. We got a small one and put it in our basement where my room was. I would lift weights and listen to Al Green's greatest hits every day, almost all day. I was young, but I guess you can say I had an old soul. While "Tired of Being Alone" played in the background, I was counting out sets, sweat dripping onto the flooded, musty floors of my basement but I was determined to get bigger, quiet the doubt, and make a name for myself. Al Green helped get me through some rough days in that basement.

As days went by at school, classmates and teachers began to notice my speed during gym class, and I was asked to try joining the track team and football team. I practiced hard and within the next two weeks, it was time for my first track meet. I was beyond nervous. I jumped out the blocks as far as I could and ran with my head down for at least fifty meters, running as fast as I could. I could hear people shouting "Go, Thig, go!" and my coach saying, "Relax your shoulders and breathe." I didn't feel anyone running alongside of me and didn't see anyone in front of me, and that's when I knew I had to be killing them. I felt like I had just accomplished a lifetime goal, but I never ever thought about running track. Running across that finish line was like running into a new destiny set ahead of me. That's a day that I will never forget. I realized things were turning around for me. To go out there and win the very first time gave me all the confidence in the world.

When football season came around, I was already known for my speed, but there were still questions of could I catch, could I take a hit? What was I like with pads on? My very first game was on JV (junior varsity). I was yet again very nervous because the guys were a lot bigger than the P.A.L. league that I played with in the last season. My first game, I put my pads on and they were huge; my pants were too big, and I borrowed some cleats from the school's shoe donation box because we couldn't afford them at the time. I earned my spot and was named the starting running back. The twin, however, was moved to linebacker, and his twin brother was the quarterback. The first play we ran was a run play to me, and when I got the ball on a twenty-six power run, I remember running through the hole, making a couple guys miss, and then eventually getting tackled. At that point, the butterflies and jitters that I had going crazy in my stomach were now flying in formation and I was ready for more action. That game, I scored three touchdowns and we won the game.

The twins and I became best friends , and we were with each other every single day. One day, twin(quarterback) told me he believed in me, and if I kept doing what I was doing, I'd for sure be in the league one day. I didn't hear that too often and those words stuck with me and quieted the small voices in my head that were quick to remind me of my past. They showed me the ropes around the school and introduced me to a lot of people. He had so much confidence in me that I was ready to go to war with him every game.

After the first few games, the twins and I were moved up to the varsity squad. I was so excited and knew that I could really do something with football and track. My heart was always with football, but track would help me with my straight-line speed and I loved it. I got back to my old ways in school and took everything we did seriously. I passed all my tests, did all my homework, asked for extra-credit work, and tried my best to do everything the right way. All was well; what more could I ask for with this amazing start to my new school?

I was starting to talk to girls and this one girl in particular was almost sort of a fatal attraction. After talking for a bit, I realized that I no longer wanted to talk to her and she said some things to me that made me over-react and call her out her name. We had a big argument in the hallway after school and she went on to say that she was going to have her brothers and cousins come up to the school and jump me for calling her out her name. I told her to have whoever she wanted to come up there and didn't care.

I would have tried to fight every last one of them by myself and didn't care if I lost or got beat up but I wasn't scared nor about to be punked by anyone. The next day it was a big crowd outside and people came to me to warn me that she had her people come up there to beat me up. I immediately got angry and saw red and my blood was pumping and my heart started pumping fast as I was making my way outside to go and fight whoever was out there.

The word that the new guy that was a football player got around the school and my teammates found out about it. It was one guy that I had never met that was known around the school that came outside in front of me and said if they fight you they have to fight all of us. I looked behind me and it was the whole football team with this guy that was smaller than me in the front. He walked up to the guys and said "who out here got a problem with my brother" No one said anything and they left after they saw us out there. I went home and told my mother about this guy that I didn't know that stood up for me and how the team came together to fight with me. She said she wanted to meet him and I had him come over and he's been like a brother to me since that day. At that moment I realized that playing football and being a part of something bigger than me was something unique and special.

One day, before practice, I saw this cheerleader around the school, and she was the most gorgeous girl I had ever seen. I was in love at first sight. I used to hear people say that they fell in love at first sight but never really believed it was possible until this day. I thought to myself, *Now you know you have a bad history with girls, are you sure you want to chance this again with all the success that you're having?* I felt that I had matured a lot within a year and was ready to have a girlfriend, but there was a problem. The problem was that she was older, and I was a bit shy. I didn't know if she had a boyfriend, and I was so intimidated by her beauty and thought she would turn me down. Now, if I were only able to talk to her and eventually get her to be my girlfriend, I would have everything I wanted. I did what a lot of young high schoolers would do—I asked my boy to hook it up for me to talk to her. When the time came, she was in her dance class and the opportunity presented itself. My boy said to her, "Joy, this is Marcus; Marcus, this is Joy." That was it. That's all you gon' give me? Okay, think, think, think. The conversation was very brief because I didn't have any game and was still in shock. I eventually asked for her number, and she wrote it on a white napkin. I still remember the number and how she wrote it. I felt complete that day. We talked, we connected, and it was perfect, so one day I finally asked her to be my girl, and of course she couldn't resist, so she said yes. I had my girl, my new crew, and was almost a 4.0 student. Football and track were going great; it felt like I was dreaming after coming out what I had gone through.

After Joy and I had been together for two years, In my mind I couldn't stop negative thoughts, *'You know this won't last forever, your girlfriend is older and she will graduate before you…what will you do then? How will you maintain that relationship with all the popularity that you have, knowing that you will be alone?* In time, Joy graduated but she didn't go to an out-of-state college, so my plan was to hold on as long as possible.

It was now my senior year and I couldn't believe I was getting letters from colleges for football and track. I started getting invites to visit different campuses with my parents to see how they were and to ultimately make a decision on where I wanted to go. As I was getting letters from a lot of small schools and just a few big schools, I was thinking to myself that Indiana University would allow me to get the exposure to take my skills to the next level—to my ultimate dream. It was a Big Ten school, and the coach who came to see me at my school and my home was a very nice man. We connected right away. This process to me was new and different; it was scary because I didn't want to leave but I knew I had to leave. I was the vice-president of the 2004 class at my high school, a team captain, an honor roll student, and was now about to get a full-ride college scholarship. This can't be my life, I thought, this can't be real. Things like this don't happen to people like me with such a dark past or no one I know for that matter. While all this was going on, there were a lot of rumors getting to Joy that I was dating someone else while she wasn't there and that I had a lot of girls. I'm sure that was hard for her because she wasn't there and had no clue of what I would be like alone. However, we talked frequently and I would promise her that I was truly committed to her. We eventually broke up after a lot of he-said, she-said, and that really set me back. I was heartbroken, and I cried to myself because this was the girl I for sure wanted to marry one day. I already had it in my plans. At any rate, things didn't look good for us. I decided to go ahead and give her space and focus on all the things I had going on in my life.

It was close to national signing day, and I was one step closer to joining an elite class; something that no one in my family had ever done. The closet to get to that level was my older cousin that I looked up to. I wanted to be just like him. He was my inspiration and the reason why I even pursued playing football. I saw the response he was getting from family and friends and I wanted that. I remember going to his games while I was young and we were all cheering him on and all I could think of is one day that will be me. He went on to a lot of camps but never went to play ball at the next level. That was the jumpstart that I needed and I thank him for leading and setting that example for me.

There were very few who did it from my high school. I would be the first to get a full ride scholarship to college or go to college period, that was unheard of in my neighborhood. Getting this scholarship would relieve all the stress of my parents having to pay for anything. The day I signed my letter of intent was one of the happiest days of my life. I sat and thought to myself, *my mom wouldn't let me play football for a long time when I was younger because I was too small, but look at where it has gotten me.* I'd always wanted this and watched it on TV and in movies, but for this to be really happening to me . . . it was all surreal. I was thinking about how I'd get to play in the Big Ten conference on national television for all of my family and friends to see. I wanted to make everyone proud and show the world what I was made of and that I wasn't defined by my mistakes.

I continued to excel in both sports and academics that year. I walked across that stage to receive my high school diploma in my burgundy robe and baby-blue tassel. I was too hype, and nobody could tell me anything. As I shook the hands of the teaching staff and heard the applause from my classmates calling out, "2004 class vice-president Marcus Thigpen," words can't explain what that moment meant to me. My future was bright, and my destiny was calling me once I made it to this point. I was one step closer to my ultimate dream, and the next step for me was to get drafted. I was on a mission to keep going, keep fighting, keep proving to myself and everyone around me that I was destined for greatness, I was made for this, and I wasn't going to stop until I did it.

End of First Quarter: Coaching Points

Perfection is not attainable, but if we chase perfection,
we can catch excellence.

—Vince Lombardi

In the game of football, you will always make mistakes; things will never be perfect. The amount of time we put in daily matters and although the goal is to attain perfection, we will have to settle for excellence. No matter how bad things are, the good news is that you never have to stay there, and once you start at the bottom, you can only rise to the top!

Sideline Reflections

"What disasters in your life have you been able to overcome?"

By reminding yourself of insurmountable odds that you've overcome in the past, you will be able to draw upon that experience for the future challenges coming your way.

The truth is - you are resilient.

A recent study shows that HALF the companies in the S&P 500, were started during times of crisis. Half! These are some of the most valuable brands anywhere in the world!

And yet, they were birthed not from good times, but from extraordinarily DIFFICULT TIMES.

These periods of great trial gave birth to companies like:

1. Procter & Gamble (Founded during the panic of 1837)
2. General Motors (Founded during the panic of 1907)
3. Fortune Magazine (Founded 90 days after the market crash of 1929)
4. Walt Disney company (A year after founding, it ran into the market crash of 1929)
5. Revlon (Founded during the Great Depression - 1932)
6. Costco (Founded during the recession of the late 1970s)
7. LinkedIn (Founded in 2002, right after the dot-com bubble)

Bottom line? The crisis isn't what defines you; your response to it is what defines you.

What disasters in your life have you been able to overcome? (They may be the same as those listed in the previous chapter).

"5 disasters I have overcome in my past are:"

1. _____

2. _____

3. _____

4. _____

5. _____

RESIST & PERSIST

2ND QUARTER
THE DEDICATION

5

SECOND DOWN

It was a long six-hour drive from Detroit, to Bloomington, Indiana, but Pops somehow got us there in one of the old cars he would spend countless hours fixing up. Every time we stopped to get gas, we had to keep the car running because we were afraid that if we turned it off, it wouldn't start again. We had that fear on top of the fear of it blowing up while pumping the gas with it on, so it was lose-lose. Sitting in the backseat of this green Lincoln, I watched my dad nervously pump the gas, and it instantly took me back down memory lane. I remember being a little kid and watching my dad and his boy, fix up all the old, run-down cars. Coming out from underneath the car, covered in black oil, his shirt and his fingernails were always black from his work. They spent so many hours talking about dreams of owning a tow-truck company. Though he never really walked me through fixing a car, just by me watching him day in and day out, I picked up on so many things that I use even now today. So as Pops finished up pumping the gas, I noticed his black fingertips, and it gave me even more determination to go and make a name for myself so he could own that business that he always dreamed of.

I walked onto campus with my mom dad and thought, Wow, I'm really here, I really made it! Seeing her smile confirmed the joy I felt, because deep down inside, I knew that, in that moment, I had erased just a little bit of the stress I'd caused her over the years. As I moved my things from the car, I couldn't help but notice the drastic difference between where I grew up and where I was now standing. Detroit was pretty rough compared to Bloomington. Everything in Bloomington was so nice and clean. Flowers covered the grounds, buildings were well kept, and the grass was so green. I knew Bloomington was a college town, and the presentation and the upkeep had to look nice to bring students in, but this was like nothing I'd ever seen before.

The cars were even different. In Detroit, most of the cars you saw were "old school" with loudspeakers in them, shaking the block. Some had the rims that spin and a nice candy paint job. In Bloomington, I didn't see any of that; people were driving luxury cars like Mercedes Benz, Cadillacs, and BMWs, and at that point I knew that they had completely different mind-sets and these were students the same age as myself.

I had never really encountered so many people of other racial and ethnic backgrounds. Being in Bloomington felt like being somewhere foreign, and I didn't know what to expect. I saw every ethnicity possible. There were Chinese, European, and Latinos, to name a few, and very few blacks. Coming from a predominantly black city to barely seeing people who looked like me, I felt a little nervous and out of place racially. For the first time, I felt like I was the minority. I'd read many stories on racism growing up, but it was such a farfetched thought because all I was accustomed to were African-American people. I never experienced it, so it was irrelevant. I didn't know if I was going to be treated differently because of the color of my skin, and this was the first time this question ever crossed my mind. All my friends would tell me that white people didn't like blacks in Indiana, so be careful, but I never paid it much attention, because I couldn't fathom how someone could hate another because of the color of his or her skin. I was naïve to the thought of that because I had never experienced it. But the faculty, staff, advisors, students, and everyone far exceeded my expectations. They were so nice and welcoming and made me feel like regardless of where I came from, I belonged there.

Sideline Reflections

By going to Indiana University, I found myself in an environment of excellence. But was this really a necessary step for my development as a football player? Absolutely.

I had the raw ingredients but I needed that environment of excellence to truly help me blossom. Unfortunately, society too often preaches that "you either have it or you don't." "You're either naturally gifted or you'll never excel."

The truth is quite different from that.

In the book "The Talent Code: Unlocking the Secret of Skill in Sports, Art, Music, Math, and Just About Anything", author Daniel Coyle shares an anecdote about Brazilian soccer (futbol).

Why do Brazilian soccer players excel at dribbling, almost universally, at a higher level than players from other countries?

It's because Brazil is a natural environment of excellence. A "Talent Hotbed", as Mr. Coyle puts it. Brazil evolved into a soccer talent hotbed (it wasn't always that way) after they adopted a version of soccer called "Futbol de Salal" or "Futsal." Futbol de Salal literally means: "Football in the living room."

Kids would play with a ball half the size of a regular ball with greater weight and less bounce. The game is played indoors on a concrete court. Or sometimes, literally in the living room. Always in a smaller space. The result is a ball that requires much more work to dribble. In fact, kids playing Futsal get SIX TIMES as many touches on the ball compared to kids playing normal soccer. Why play with more difficult rules and more restrictions?

Because adversity breeds excellence.

Pursue comfort and you will find yourself mired in mediocrity.

Strive to be uncomfortable, particularly under the direction of an expert mentor or coach, and you will max out your abilities.

Look through your life. At what times have you been in an environment of excellence?

Now look at your current life today.

What do you need to excel in? Where can you find that environment of success?

"In the past, the top 3 Environments of Excellence I have been in were:"

1. _____

2. _____

3. _____

"Looking at my current goals, 3 Environments of Excellence I need to get to over the next few years, are:"

1. _____

2. _____

3. _____

6
FALSE START

There's a popular saying that goes, "If you're early, then you are on time; if you're on time, you are late; and if you're late, then you are forgotten." I went through a lot to get to college, and now that I was finally here, forgotten was the last thing I was going to be. At 5:45 a.m., my alarm clock went off and almost scared me half to death. All I could think was, *this is not what I signed up for!* But it was day one of training camp, not just on a collegiate level for me. I needed to prepare for the professional level. I wasn't used to structure, timed meetings, having to be where I was expected when they told me to, or getting up early. We had a few guys who showed up late and one guy who missed the bus and had to catch a ride with an upperclassman because when the bus departs, there's no remorse.

We had to get physicals, and when I heard that, I was prepared to give a urine sample and check my vital signs, cool I've had a few of these before. This physical was a top-of-the-line physical: we had to get an EKG, meet with a foot specialist, take x-rays of any previous injuries, fill out what felt like a thousand forms and get dental and vision tests. We had breakfast, and then we went on to the first team meeting. We all had to stand up one by one and tell our names, where we were from and what position we played. Coach went on to give us house rules, what to expect and what our goals were as a team. Then we were given a playbook and were expected to know a certain amount of plays for the next day because we were going to run them in practice, and it was up to us to know what we were doing out there. This playbook looked like a dictionary; it was so thick with what seemed like a million plays. We didn't even have a playbook in high school, we had a few pieces of paper with a few plays on them and that was it. We weren't as advanced; we watched film maybe once or twice a week, if that. Growing up in Detroit, we had raw talent but no fundamentals or structure, we just ran the few plays that had been around for decades. Here, I learned quickly that every day was an evaluation, and this was another step to me becoming a better player and getting to the next level.

Our days were so long and it took me a few days to get adjusted to this new lifestyle. We would wake up at 5:45 a.m to go and get breakfast, then head to meetings, then we would get dressed for our first practice. After practice, we would go watch the film from practice to make corrections, then to lunch. We would have a break for two hours, then it would be time for more meetings before our next practice. We would go from the second practice to dinner then to night meetings. When we were done, it would be close to 9:30pm and its time for bed to wake up and do it all over again. This was every single day, unless we had an day off which was very rare. This schedule to me was shocking and demoralizing at the same time. I was exhausted daily and all I wanted to do was sleep.

Camp was coming to an end and I made some great strides and a great impression on the coaching staff and came out healthy. I remember the first day I got on campus after a hard-fought training camp and being with all my teammates grinding. We had a welcome-back block party on the street where the dorms were. My teammates and I were so happy to see other faces and have some freedom. The feeling of breaking camp, if I had to compare it to something, would be like being free after a month long punishment of being locked up in your room, coming out only to eat and use the restroom and do homework. I was walking around, smiling, excited to start this new phase of my life and ready to see where I was going to be staying and with whom. The school environment was a very friendly place overall. Things were set up in such a way that it was easy to find, although the campus was huge. Classes were set up like we were in an auditorium; the classes weren't so small and personal anymore. I was in class with about one hundred other students, so there was no more one-on-one time with the teacher.

For that, you had to go to the professor's office during their office hours, which were listed on the syllabus. The syllabus was given to every student on the first day of class, and it explained what we would be doing for the whole year, what books to get, what to read, what needed to be completed, and so on. The professors throw all of what you need right at you on the first day. It's a bit much, but if you follow it and stay on top of everything that's in there, it makes things a lot easier. We didn't have these in high school so this was also new for me. I didn't know what a syllabus was.

My roommate and I, after moving our things into our room, decided we wanted to go around and do some mingling and meet people. Everyone had booths out with all types of brochures for different programs, all type of fraternities, sororities, credit card booths, and so on. Music was playing over the loudspeakers and I thought to myself, this is more like it.

I had no idea what to do, who to sign up with, or anything. I was so overwhelmed for a moment because I didn't want to miss out on an opportunity that could benefit me in the future. But I didn't have my mother to tell me what to do like she usually did, and I didn't know what half of the stuff was, so I stayed away from most of it and just looked around. I came across one both that had people signing up for credit cards. I had never had a credit card, and didn't know anything about credit or how it worked. I know I liked the sound of having a credit card and being able to spend money on necessities. This was different from anything I'd ever been a part of. In high school, everything was already set up for me and I never had to make these type of decisions.

Thankfully, people really cared about our well-being. They wanted to know what our backup plans were, what we would do if football ended today . . . questions that really made me think. I was asked this by a few of the people who lived in our dorms. I had people taking time out of their day to help me study because I had no idea how to study at this level. When you get to a major university, you can't just read one book and get all your answers. You have to do real research and compare and contrast, and that's one thing I learned living in the dorms with people who were experienced.

I didn't have too many bad experiences in the dorms. They were very clean for the most part. We had a community restroom, which was well maintained. The only thing I didn't like was that we couldn't bring anyone over without everyone being in our business. Overall the dorm life was fun. People were actually there to help each other out. I don't know if it was because I played football or not, but everyone was so caring and nice and made my experience a fun one. Having a roommate was really dope at times because we could play video games whenever we wanted, talk about life, study together if we had the same class or just go hoop at the recreation center together. Then other times, it could be challenging and made me want to live alone and never have a roommate.

There were times when my socks, tank tops, and even underwear would come up missing, and I know he had my stuff on, but he wouldn't admit to it. I was shorter, but we wore the same size, so I started to lock my things up. Every time I confronted him, he would deny it, so I decided to move in with someone else without even telling him, after many close calls and confrontations. I had been planning it for a while. I told my teammate, all the things that was happening, and he didn't have a roommate, so he told me that I could come and move in with him. He was three hundred pounds and one of the coolest people I have met , and I knew he wouldn't be able to fit my stuff or steal from me. He could steal my snacks, though, because he was a big fella. He also stayed in a coed dorm, so that was a plus for me too coming from an all-boys dorm. When my old roommate wasn't there, my other teammate came over and helped me move my things across the street with him. The room was a lot bigger, so we didn't have bunk beds—we broke it down to two twin-size beds. This dorm also had the food court connected to it, and this restaurant called the Underground that we used to go to was right next door. I had more privacy over there with him, and none of my clothes came up missing. We clicked and connected from day one. My other roommate was cool with it because he liked being alone, too, so it worked out for the both of us.

There were never any hard feelings between us, but I just had to get myself out of that situation before things got any worse.

Sideline Reflections

Getting to the Environment of Excellence was the beginning of a quantum leap for me. I was finally getting some structure. I was in a place where high expectations were being placed on me and not just athletically.

For the first time, talent was not enough. I could no longer rely on raw athleticism. I had to study plays. I had to wake up early. I learned the true definition of what it was to be disciplined.

The late Jim Rohn has a quote that illustrates this aptly.

"Discipline weighs ounces. Regret weighs tons." Discipline isn't fun but its results sure are.

Hard work without expert guidance sure gets you farther than kicking back and being lazy.

But it doesn't get you ALL THE WAY.

An expert coach can facilitate what Daniel Coyle's "The Talent Code" and Geo Colvin's "Talent is Overrated," refer to as Error-Focused Practice... or Deep Practice.

This kind of practice is like none other because as opposed to focusing on: Simply doing practice...

Or even focusing on doing practice hard...

It focuses on doing practice RIGHT.

Error-Focused Practice is maddeningly frustrating. It is full of starts and stops as the coach corrects every basic movement. It is not fun to watch either.

But if you can find an Environment of Excellence, and within it find a coach that will facilitate Error-Focused Practice (Deep Practice) with you, you will slowly develop into an unstoppable force. This is scientifically proven, in disciplines as wide-ranging as Sports, Art, Music, and Math. It flat-out works.

How many of these would you say are sometimes true about you?

1. "I hate failing."
2. "I love failing."
3. "If I fail at something, it means I'm not good at it."
4. "I don't accept failure."
5. "Failure is a part of life. There's nothing I can do about it."
6. "I want to fail as much as possible."
7. "Failure is for losers."
8. "I procrastinate to delay an inevitable failure."
9. "I want to avoid failure as much as I can… but if it happens I deal with it."
10. "If I fail too much, it affects my self-esteem."

Fill in your thoughts about failure, in your own words.

_____

_____

_____

Who have been your toughest coaches to date - in any arena of life?

And what did you learn?

Coach/Mentor 1: _____

What I learned: _____

_____

Coach/Mentor 2: _____

What I learned: _____

_____

Coach/Mentor 3: _____

What I learned: _____

_____

7
SIDELINE INFRACTION

I was called to my coach's office as the season was closing in, and I was told that I was being redshirted because they had a senior running back and a sophomore ahead of me. Also, they wanted me to develop more, learn the system and to put on some weight. After hearing this, I didn't know what to expect or what was next at this point. This meant that I was a part of the team, but I wasn't going to play that year unless there was an emergency where guys got hurt and they needed me to step in. After that, things started to go downhill for me in the classroom. I was upset because I had expected to play that year and have my family and friends come down to see me, so that really took a toll on me.

There were a lot of students who went to my high school who were prepared for college by the way they handled business. They would study for hours, go to libraries, have study sessions, and were on top of it. I was naïve and had no idea that it would be that way. I didn't know anyone that went to college, I never had a mentor outside of football, so I had to learn everything on my own. In my family, no one went to college, so I didn't have anyone to turn to for help.

I did enough to know what I needed to know, but I wouldn't do anything extra. I can count on one hand how many times I went to the library in high school, whereas I was going almost every single day in college. In high school, everyone was out for him- or herself and not too worried about the next person except for close friends. In college, people were offering to help me. I assumed I looked like I was lost.

In college, you could have two classes one day a week and have the whole day free, and you had to know how to manage your time. A lot of my free time was spent trying to nap or study. High school courses and teachers for sure prepared me for college with some of the things that we learned, especially in the advanced classes, but as for how much freedom I had in college, high school couldn't prepare me for that.

You have to come home to your parents daily in high school, whereas in college you are grown, have your own place, have your own car, cook your own meals, and wash and fold your own clothes. It's just you, with no one to help or call because everyone is so far away if you go away to school. It grows you up a lot and allows you to mature to new levels faster than most.

I started skipping class, sleeping in, and going to practice as if nothing happened with school. I started partying with my teammates and staying out late nights and drinking. I played video games instead of studying, talking on the phone and really not caring. No one ever knows if you go to class or not until the assignments show up not turned in, you miss a test, or you ultimately fail the course. I was at a point where I was starting to fail a few classes, and we had to have a certain GPA to be eligible to play football. Once our grades came out, they were sent to the coaching staff as well, and I was called in to my running back coach's office, the man who took me under his wing as if I were his own son. He showed me my grades in disappointment because he knew I was better than that. He expected way more out of me. He told me that as a staff, they had decided I was going to be on academic probation until I brought my grades up. I knew that I could do the work, but I let my getting redshirted get the best of me. That was my excuse for letting go, but while talking with my coach, he told me that if I didn't get my grades up, my scholarship would be taken away from me, and I would have to go back home. The last thing I wanted to do was taste a little bit of success in college with it all paid for, and then go back to the hood and explain to everyone that I was back home because I couldn't keep up my grades, after being one of the smartest kids in the city. This was a turning point for me, and I'm glad it happened earlier rather than later.

I never told my mom or anyone—and she still doesn't know to this day— so when she would call and check on me, I would say everything was good and that my grades were good. But she could very well be coming back to pick me up if I didn't get it right. I knew I had time to get it right and she wouldn't have a clue what my grades looked like. We didn't get report cards anymore; everything was online, and my mom didn't know what was going on. To her, I was as innocent as a brand-new baby. I had to adjust my schedule; trying to figure out how I would get everything done was really the hardest part of school for me. I know I chose to play sports and go to school, but being a student athlete was a tough task, especially as a freshman trying to adjust. My schedule went like this: Wake up at 5:45 a.m. to go get a morning workout with the team; we had to lift weights and run. We usually got done with that at around 6:30 a.m. Now I had to shower, get dressed, get to mandatory breakfast, eat, and then get on the bus to get to my 8:00 a.m. class. We, as athletes, usually took four to five classes between 8:00 a.m. and 3:00 p.m., hopefully with a lunch in between because right after classes we had to hustle back to the stadium for meetings and practice. We would practice until 5:30 or 6:30 p.m. By then, I was exhausted and wanting to lie down, but I couldn't because we had mandatory dinner and study hall, where we had to log hours in weekly and study with tutors to get our work done. By the time I got back to the dorm, it was dark out; the day was pretty much over and I still needed to study. This really took a toll on my body, my mind, and my relationships. I couldn't talk on the phone like I used to, I couldn't play video games the way I used to, I was often too tired to do anything extra and would just go to sleep. Most nights I would lie in bed and wonder what it would be like to be a regular student where I could go to classes only, spread them out as I pleased, come home, take naps and study and get an advantage and be prepared for tests. My mind was so tired that when it was time to study, I couldn't focus and would be dozing off. I couldn't take the major I initially wanted, which was engineering, because I had to make my schedule around my football schedule. The classes I needed for that major conflicted, so I had to change my major. I was a student athlete, and I thought student was before athlete but, in most cases, you're an athlete before a student because you're on an athletic scholarship. My relationship with my mom, my friends back home, and family members started to become nonexistent because I would be too tired to talk. When I'd come home, I needed time to myself, and when I got that time, I usually watched my favorite TV show, Martin, until I fell asleep.

My mom would often say to me, "You can't be that tired," and after I'd tell her about my days, she would say she understood. But I know she didn't; all she wanted to do was talk, but I couldn't even do that for her. I was secretly failing and was under a lot of pressure to get myself back on track so I wouldn't get sent back home. I had to sacrifice a lot to make sure I didn't miss out on this very rare opportunity that I was given.

My first year was coming to an end, and although I didn't play, it was a success—with a little scare, but I knew what to expect now. We had some time off for the holidays, and I knew when we got back, it was back to business as usual. My relationships back home with my friends who didn't go to college had also become nonexistent. We all went our separate ways after graduating high school; some people took advantage of their opportunities while they were there, and others went to the street life. When I would come home, I would see people I went to high school with on corners hustling and making it a way of life and it hurt me to see it, knowing the potential they had and where they were at that point. We would speak whenever we crossed paths, and they always supported and followed me and were proud to say they knew me and went to school with me. My close friends who went to college and the ones I stayed in touch with were always talking to me via social media, very rarely on cell phones. Not many people from my high school went away to college; the majority stayed in the state and went to Michigan, Michigan State, Central Michigan ,or Eastern Michigan University. I wanted to stay in state and go to school with them but those schools didn't offer me a scholarship, so I went to where I was wanted. Those were the top schools so when we had breaks and would come home, I would see them and catch up, but when I went back to school we lost touch because we all were on our grind, trying to get our degrees and be successful in life.

Back at IU, we were preparing for the spring ball and had practices up until that point. By this time I was off probation and was number one on the depth chart. The sophomore running back transferred to a new school because he didn't like the coaching staff. The senior we had was graduating, so I was next up and I was ready for this opportunity.

We got a new coaching staff and head coach but I still had my running-back coach with whom I had a solid relationship with, so I was happy about that. Our bond was growing stronger. He kept me under his wing like I was the son that he never had. When he came to my high school to recruit me, we had a few talks that allowed me to feel an immediate connection to him. Coach came to my home, sat in our living room, and talked with my mom, telling her that he wanted me at IU to be the starting running back and returner one day. My mom took to him very well, too, and we knew instantly that this was going to be a good fit for me. When he coached us, he also gave life lessons and advice, and I took it all in because I needed to hear those things from a man and not always from my mom. He didn't treat me like a player but like a son, and I respected him for instilling those things in us.

Each day in camp, I was finishing every drill in first place. I was the fastest, pound for pound the strongest for my size, and made amazing plays every day in practice. Not only were things looking up for me on the depth chart, but I was no longer as shy and reserved as I was the year before. I met my best friend to this day through the game of football. One day after practice he asked if he could come over and chill. At first I thought, What? Why does he want to come over my crib? We always joked around in meetings and at practice but I always stayed to myself. I was cool with it and told him he could come. I warned him that I didn't have anything in my apartment; I told him I didn't have a couch, no food or anything yet, just a twin air mattress that sat halfway deflated and barely making it on my living-room floor with my TV and video game. When he said, "That's cool!" I knew from that point on, he was going to be my boy. We sat on the air mattress while drinking wine coolers, playing the video game, played cards, shared our hopes and dreams of the future and where we had come from. I realized we had a lot in common and he was a true genuine person. He became more than a friend, he was now a brother and I was able to meet his family and he was able to meet mine. This was me stepping outside my comfort zone for the first time and it was a blessing to have him in my corner.

As we were getting closer to our first game at home, I was so nervous because I was a starter. Although I was ready and earned the position I was in, I was a little shaken because it was now time for me to showcase my talents in front of our 65,000-seat stadium, when I was used to playing in front of one to two hundred people max in high school. The night before the game that kicked off my sophomore season, we had meetings, going over the game plan and what it was going to take to beat our opponent.

I was taking notes and visualizing myself scoring as soon as I touched the ball. I sat there in meetings visualizing myself having one of the best games a player could have. After meetings we had a snack which was chips, cookies, and ice cream with sprinkles and that helped with my nerves a bit. I went to my room and watched a game that was on from some teams that played earlier, and the butterflies started moving even faster because I knew that when I went to sleep and woke up, it was about to be game time and there was no turning back. I got on my knees, said my prayers, and went to bed. I laid there tossed and turned and couldn't get any sleep. I was so nervous and it wasn't even game time yet. I kept replaying my coach words, seeing the plays in my playbook, and thinking about taking my first hit. I thought about what it would be like to step out there between those lines in front of all those people, with my teammates depending on me. I finally fell asleep and I felt like I was sleep at most maybe an hour before my alarm went off and it was time to get up, get ready to eat breakfast and head to the bus to be taken to the stadium.

We all looked ready in our crimson and cream jogging suits. Everybody had on head-phones, and it was silent. We were game ready and in game mode. We did a new walk to the stadium, where we walked through the tailgating area with all our fans led by the band, and then we walked to the stadium and into the locker room. That walk was short but had us so hyped and ready to interact with our support system before the game. It was the best feeling in the world. People were calling my name and doing Thigpen chants, and they hadn't even seen me play yet. In my mind, I couldn't let them down. I had to put on a show for my fans and for the team to win. I finally got to the locker room where everything was nicely placed in our lockers: jerseys with our names on them, pants, cleats, gloves, wristbands, and so on. It was time to strap up. Everything was nice and tight, just how I liked it. We did our warmups and came back in before kickoff for our pregame speech. As we walked out of the locker room, the crowd got so loud that it shocked me. I caught myself looking up and looking around in amazement to be playing at this level, and I immediately started thanking God. We won the coin toss, and I knew that I would soon get some action on the field after our returner received the kick. We ran out on the field after the return and it was time for action. I was shaking a bit, but I knew in my mind that I was well prepared for this. I was most nervous about the hits. I had no idea what to expect from these guys. We did some hitting in camp, but this was different because these guys weren't my teammates, and I knew that they were going to try to light me up. First play of the game was a run play and I got the ball and took off up the middle for about five yards before I got my first hit. I took that hit and said to my teammates, "That's it?" Oh, it's on now, I just needed to get that out of my system. We ran the ball again and I got a gain of twenty yards. Now, I was feeling myself spinning the ball and trying to show some swagger. We passed the ball down the field for a big gain of about forty yards, the crowd was so loud and excited. We were now in the red zone and I was anxious to get in the end zone. We ran a toss to the outside and it was a race to the pylon. It was me and the defender, and I was determined to win. I got the ball and saw that I had some great blocks, so I ran to the outside and ran as fast as I could to the corner and I was in. My first game at the collegiate level, my first touchdown, and that feeling of joy, pain, setbacks, flashes of the accident, the ups and downs I had been through up until that point—it all came back and I wanted to cry as I crossed the goal line. I took a knee, thanked my heavenly Father, and went and celebrated with my teammates. We went on to win the game. I scored another touchdown against the Indiana State defense that was a long sixty-yard run as well. I ended the game with ten carries for 130 yards, and we blew them out. I got the game ball from my coach, and I started to get buzz around campus as people were starting to notice who I was and that I played football. I always tried to stay out of sight on campus and not around often. My coach would give us life lessons every meeting, and one saying that really stuck with me was, "You can't be a superstar and be accessible to everyone. You have to make people want to see you." I think that was his way of telling us not to go out and party and to stay in our books and have fun sparingly. I was staying on top of my grades and everything was going really well.

Sideline Reflections

"If a player's not doing the things he should,
put him on the bench. He'll come around."

- John Wooden.

Being redshirted had to be a serious blow for a proud, talented, and accomplished young athlete like Marcus.

While we've often been "redshirted" in our own lives, the truth is that it happens to the best of us. Even the most successful people in society, in history, have been redshirted.

Don't believe me?

Theodore Roosevelt was born in 1858. A sickly child, he was often unable to play outside, or go to school.

Teddy suffered debilitating asthma. Doctors didn't understand the disease very well at the time, and Teddy was prescribed such remedies as going on vacation to the coast, smoking cigars, and drinking coffee and whiskey. (Seriously).

By age twelve, he suffered nightly near-death asthma attacks.

His father resolved to teach him to build his body.

"Theodore," his father said, "you have the mind, but don't have the body. I'm going to teach you to develop your body. It's going to be hard drudgery but I think you have the determination."

Theodore responded with his trademark determination: "I'll MAKE my body."

So for the next five years, he lifted weights and worked out daily in his father's homemade gym. They frequently went mountain-climbing together.

Teddy became a strapping and hearty young man, taking up competitive boxing and rowing as a student at Harvard.

He became governor of New York state, Vice-President of the United States, and the youngest President of the United States at age forty-two. His love of nature led him to establish 150 national forests, five national parks, and eighteen national monuments.

"A setback is a setup for a major comeback." Author Unknown

In what arena of life would you say that you've been "redshirted" - told you're not good enough?

"In the past, I've been told I wasn't good enough in these three arenas:"

1. _____

2. _____

3. _____

How have you responded in the past to being told you weren't good enough?

_____

How would you like to respond to being "redshirted" in your life, going forward?

_____

_____

_____

8
SUBSTITUTION

Our starting kick returner was a senior and was smaller than me. I really wanted to play his position but he had great prior years and had earned his stripes. I always tried to steal knowledge from the older guys, and there was one guy in particular, Lance, whom I looked up to. I always felt like if he could do it, then I could as well. I remember asking him what made him different? How did he stand out and be so good at what he did? He was a ghostwriter with his brothers for celebrity rap artists as well, and he could rap. I was expecting something like, "I study a lot, I run extra sprints, or I do extra sets in the weight room." He told me, "I have a spiritual relationship with Jesus Christ, and that's how I'm blessed with these abilities." I wanted what he had and wanted to be like him because watching his highlights had me excited to do that too. I wanted to be an instant spark and score long ninety-six-yard touchdowns on returns like he did. I was lost for words and didn't know how to react to that, and I could only remember my mother speaking of God and what he could do but I haven't experienced these things myself yet, so the first thing I said was, "okay, how do I become a Christian?" He responded, "It's simple, Thig, It's a relationship and not religion so don't get that confused. He went on to tell me that this decision was something that I should do research on and study before I make the decision. He also told me that it would change me from the inside out and it would be one of the most important decisions that I would make. I was ready and asked what the next steps were and asked him if he could bring me to salvation. He agreed and said all you have to do is repeat after me." He told me all I had to do was believe with my heart and confess with my mouth that there is only one true living God, and that was all it took.

He went on to teach me more about my new relationship and how it's not religion. I was so excited, I felt different instantly. I felt like I was a part of something and like a gate of opportunity and possibilities opened up for me the moment I repeated his words. I had chill bumps on my arms as I really began to feel God's presence and His love consume me from the inside out. And from that day forward, things started changing in my favor. Lance and I would have our own bible studies that later grew to include a few more teammates who joined in on the studies. Lance, or Flo, as we called him, was deeply rooted in the Word and could break down scriptures in a way that made it easy for me, a new believer, to understand. It was like a whole new world. I developed a thirst for learning more about my new relationship with Christ. I would always pray to God but never understood what I was doing or that I needed a relationship with him. I was growing and maturing in every aspect of my life at this point.

We were in our fourth game of the season, and my boy, Lance, hurt his knee. He had bad knees and I was his backup. I walked up to him while he was on the bike on the sideline to warm his legs up and checked on him. He instantly laid his hand on my shoulder and said a quick prayer for me before I went out to do his kick return duty as if he knew that he was about to pass the torch on to me. I remember going out there a little hesitant because this was my first time back, and even though I'd done this before in high school and always wanted to do it, now it was really time and I knew I had to make a great impression. The kick was up in the air, it seemed like forever before it dropped.

I was trying to stay focused on timing up the ball, watching the other team running down the field at me and then back at the ball again. Here it comes. I caught it and like a movie I "zoned out" and silenced the crowd in my mind, and all I remember seeing were people running at me full speed. I saw some of my teammates get knocked down while others were knocking the other team's players down, and finally I saw a window that opened up for me.

My teammate accidentally ran into me while he was trying to block for me but I was running so fast that I almost beat him to the spot and we bounced off one another. I bumped off him and kept going; he went to block a guy from my right while I was running and all I saw was green grass and the kicker and I wasn't about to get tackled by the kicker. I put a move on the kicker and ran as fast as I could without looking back. My chest was pounding, the crowd was getting loud, and I felt like I was back on the track, in my first track meet running as fast as I could. Trying to relax, but breathing rapidly I came up on the twenty yard line . . . the ten . . . no one was near me, and there was my first touchdown as a kick returner, my first time ever being back there. I felt unstoppable and was enjoying every moment of it. I ran back to the sideline and all of my teammates including Lance all came and congratulated me—happy to see me doing well because they knew how hard I worked to get to that point.

I remained humble through it all, and at this point I felt like I had everything I needed and wanted. I had my apartment, I had good grades, and my season was going well but I was missing Joy from high school and wanted to be able to share my success with her. I finished the season as one of the top five kick returners and broke numerous school records. I was starting to get calls from agents. I met a few boosters who were trying to buy me things but I saw what happened to people who got caught, so I never accepted anything and I started hearing things about the draft and predictions on where I could go if I kept playing the way I played.

As the phenomenal season I was having continued, it was time for one of the biggest games thus far in my college career. It was November 13, 2006, on an early Saturday afternoon when we met Michigan State on our turf. What was so special about this game to me was that Michigan was home for me, and State was the school I always wanted to play for. I had even gone on an unofficial visit to meet the staff, view the facility, and see what it would be like if I were to be offered to play there. That all, unfortunately, ended when State's scout told me that I was smaller than they thought and I wouldn't be a good fit for the program because of my size. That was a blow to the chest for me because I knew that despite my size, I had potential to do great things but I couldn't get them to believe in me. That brings us to the moment where I put on my game jersey, spatted up my cleats, and got ready to walk onto the field to prove, not only to myself but also to Michigan State and everyone else who had ever told me what I couldn't do in my life, that I wouldn't let my size define who I was or was not. This day was the day to make them regret never seeing my full potential on the field. The thing that set me apart from most was what I been through up until that point. I always came across reporters and people in general that would quickly judge me based off my size. What they didn't see was the pain that I had to endure, the near death experiences I faced, the cold and sleepless nights that I took to the field with me every game and thought of daily. My driving force was more than what the eye could ever possibly see. I had to win within.

As we prepared for the game, I was one of the players on their "players to watch for" list. They were aware of my big play-making abilities and had to conjure up a plan to stop me, how ironic. As we lined up on the field, man to man, the ball was snapped and it was a handoff. As I pocketed the ball, I saw a seam open up the middle and I ran through fast, made one of the linebackers miss his tackle, and nothing but green was in front of me.

I looked over to my left and saw the safety closing in on my heels but there was no way he was going to catch me. It was no catching me when I got to the open field; that was my mind-set. "Touchdown Thigpen!" I went down to what was now my signature one-knee kneel, and the IU band and crowd went crazy. As the sound of the Hoosiers Fight Song, "Indiana, Indiana, we're all for you . . ." echoed across the field, I couldn't believe it. But I had to keep my composure and not get lost in the hype; I had more football to play and three more quarters ahead of me. "Stay in the moment, Thig," I said to myself.

Later on that quarter, while in the red zone, it was my will against theirs. I got the handoff and had to punch it into the end zone. It was unusual for me to be in this particular play because the coaches liked to use the bigger backs to gun it in, but I was in and I didn't let them down. Touchdown number three against the school that told me I was too small to play. We ended up losing that game to State, but I had an outstanding performance—and one of my most memorable—games. I ended that year on a high with more touchdowns than I remember. Going into camp the following year as a junior, I was no longer trying to prove myself; I was now on a new mission because I knew what it took to have success at this level, and I was trying to do whatever it took to secure my place in the NFL draft in the next couple of years.

That same year, I began to run track as well. My roommate, a good friend of mine, suggested that I run track. He told me I had wheels and that I'd be good at it. So I went to talk to the indoor track coach about joining the team, but they needed to clear it with my football coach first. Coach Hoeppner (the head football coach) approved my participation in track, saying that it would help my speed, and because he was a dual sport athlete in college himself, he believed I could handle the load now that I had proven myself worthy in the classroom as well on the field. His only request was that I didn't get hurt. So it was on now.

My track practices were really light because I had just finished football season. My first track meet was two weeks after I started practicing. I was running the sixty-meter dash, two hundred meter dash, and the four-by-two-hundred-meter relay in the meet. There had to be at least four to five other colleges at this meet, which was held at our home track. I remember a lot of the guys on my track team being mad that I was able to run and be a two-sport athlete; they made it their mission to not let a football dude out run them. So there I was on a mission again with a chip on my shoulder, ready to prove to everyone, even my own teammates, that I deserved to be there, too. They had full-ride track scholarships, so to them I had no place on the track team.

It was time to get dressed for this meet and I put on the one-piece track uniform. I warmed up really well and then it was time to step into our starting blocks. I did a few jumps, touched my mom's tattoo on my left shoulder, and got into my position as they called out "On your mark." I put my head down to let them know I was ready, as all the runners have to do that to let them know we are ready to race. "Set" everybody rises up, waiting patiently for the gun to pop. Pow! I rose up and took off and tried to remember all that my high school coach had taught me. It was a very short race, and I finished with a time of 6.85 seconds. I won that race.

Now to the next one, the two hundred meter. I noticed all of my football teammates in the stands cheering for me. I had a bit of a rest in between races. I went to kick it with my boys until it was time to run again. Time came to warm up and get ready for the second race. Back to the blocks, waiting for the bang, and "Pow!" Won that race, too, with a time of 21.7 seconds. I couldn't believe I was competing at this level the way I was. I was way more comfortable and confident running track than I was with football. I had a lot of experience and exposure in track due to how successful my team was in high school. We traveled all over the world, winning races as a team, so I was mentally and physically prepared to run past anybody who tried me. There was a teammate who told everyone that I couldn't run faster than him and would never beat him. At this point, I had beaten him in the sixty and the two hundred and, ironically, I had to run with him in the four-by-two-hundred relay. We were a team of four and I was the anchor leg. We won that race, too, and after this meet and proving him wrong, we became pretty good friends. I had a really good track year; we went from indoor to outdoor. I broke a few track records as well. There was one indoor meet that was a sixty-yard dash for the Big Ten Championship. I came in third to a runner from Michigan and one from Ohio State.

I finished with a 6.77, which happened to be the fastest time in IU history in a long time.

Things were going well for me, so much so that it all felt surreal and like I was in a dream. My spiritual relationship was growing as well. Of course I was always fighting against odds, but the opportunities I had and the success I've had up until then was nothing short of a miracle for a boy who came from nothing. This year, I had my cousin move to Indiana with me because we were extremely close growing up and I wanted a better life for him. Even though I didn't have it all together myself, I was excelling on the field and the classroom and I wanted him to experience a better life than what he would see on a daily basis. He accepted my offer to come down and almost immediately got a job working at Mcdonald's.

Some things that a lot of college athletes deal with is the struggle when it comes to finances. I can speak for myself and a lot of other athletes that dealt with similar issues. We have full ride scholarships and though we don't have to pay for school, we don't have any extra money to buy everyday necessities. On the outside looking in, one would look at us as if we are spoiled because we get our books and tuition taken care of, we get meals daily but like everyone else we have bills to pay and everyday living expenses. I was able to get financial aid because my parents income fit the criteria and made me eligible to receive it. With this came stipulations, as I had to send most of the money I received back home because my mother still struggled and always being selfless and wanting to help out, would put myself in situations where I would go without lights, or heat to make sure she was good.

Being in these situations put me in some pretty tough spots and at times I was so desperate for money to get things that I needed that I messed up my credit by using that credit card I got my freshman year to the max and getting a couple more and doing the same to those.

When those got declined my cousin and I reverted to trying to steal things, rob people, and use other people cards for the things we needed. Looking back at some of the things we did and hearing of stories of young players stealing I can relate because I was that guy.

It's extremely hard to make it as an athlete of any sport especially if you don't have any financial support from family. This is no way an excuse to steal but I can understand why we did these things. It's the survival of the toughest mindset and all the things I grew up seeing in Detroit were starting to manifest on campus. I was fortunate to never get caught doing my dirt and was able to get by. We couldn't get jobs during the school year because of our schedule and I would always sit there and pray and wish I came from a family that had money or even a business. I was in college with no job, no money, credit was bad and every dime I would get I would send most back home for my family. I had no option but to make it to the NFL because I thought all my problems would go away.

I never learned about credit cards and what they could do to your credit, so when it was time to get a new apartment I was getting denied by everyone. These were some of the things that I learned along the way through experiencing denials. I was finally approved by an apartment complex and moved in right away. I was a week away from having to leave my old place and it worked out perfectly for me to move. I was barely making ends meet and my cousin and I did a lot of bad things to stay afloat but we knew we needed to stop and live our lives the right way. We changed our ways after having some long talks and almost getting caught a few times.

Sideline Reflections

"The greatest good you can do for another is not just to share your riches, but to reveal to him his own."

— Benjamin Disraeli

Rather than get mad that someone else had the position I wanted, I became friends with Lance and asked him for his secret to success. He was not only forthcoming with the secret, but he knew he was training his replacement. Lance's mentorship was key to my development - not just in football but in life as well.

Some years back, a similar thing happened with Jim, then the CEO of a small advertising company.

Believe it or not, Jim, the CEO, wanted to one day be a novelist. So despite his demanding executive job, Jim would get up before dawn and write for four hours before work. Every day.

For years, Jim continued this bizarre pursuit. A few friends and family supported his books but nothing really big happened. Then one day on a flight, Jim suddenly blurted out: "I figured it out! How to write a bestseller!"

He had finally discovered the blueprint: Given the pace of life these days, most people would probably prefer to read short chapters with a cool twist at the end of every one. He used that blueprint to write the thriller "Along Came a Spider," the first of 110 New York Times bestsellers he's had to date. A record that made him, James Patterson, the world's current #1 author, with 305 million readers worldwide.

Who in your profession would you say has the "Secret to Success?"

_____

How can you understudy them so that when your chance comes, you'll be ready?

_____

_____

When times are hard what are some productive things you can do if you don't have time to work or have no finances you can get from family?

_____

9
ILLEGAL HIT

When playing ball, sometimes you take an unexpected hit. It catches you off guard, knocks the wind out of you, but you have to take the hit like a man, be strong, and fight through the pain. The end of July rolled around again, and it was time for training camp my junior year.

We had an emergency team meeting one day that I'll never forget. There's usually some life-changing or profound lesson being taught in our meetings, but these words shook the core of the entire team that year. That meeting, Coach Hep informed us that he had a brain tumor, and no one knew the severity of it, but hearing him say that was very scary. He was always in great spirits and never seemed to show signs of pain, hurt, or that he was even battling anything. As time went on, we started to notice his hair slowly thinning. I admired his strength and how he didn't let it faze him. He implemented a lot of new and exciting things to the program, for example "The Rock," which was a large boulder placed in the stadium that the whole team would touch on our way into the stadium before each game. IU's signature "Walk" that the players would take before each game, led by a crowd of fans, was also his doing and it still goes on today. He gave me a chance to play the sport I love so much when not many people wanted to give me that same opportunity. Coach Hep played a huge role in all of our lives, so it was very hard and saddening to watch him go through this. His whole mantra was for us to play

"13," which meant go to a Bowl Game. It had been at least fourteen years since our school had made it to a Bowl Game. Coach Hep got the entire team bracelets that said "Play 13" which reminded us of our goal. The season went on as usual, and we played our hearts out for him. Around our fifth game into the season, we were told that Coach Hep had passed away.

The news had us all very saddened and questioning how this could happen to such a great man with so much potential for a program that struggled so many years. We made it our job to fight through, play hard, and ball out every game to get him that Bowl Game he always believed we could make.

Sideline Reflections

"Death leaves a heartache no one can heal.
Love leaves a memory no one can steal."

- from a headstone in Ireland.

What do you do when life catches you off guard with a vicious hit? I had already lost La'Crecia at age 14, multiple family members along the way. Now, I'd just lost my coach. Why?

Coach Hep is indelibly a part of my life story.

Who have you loved and lost that was an indelible part of your life story? And how will their memory continue to affect your life story?

Name: _____

What they meant to me: _____

_____

Name: _____

What they meant to me: _____

_____

10
THIRD DOWN

As I dealt with losing my head coach and trying to keep my head in the game, I was confused as to why these things happen to such amazing people. I had so much going on at the time and just wanted someone to share it with, and I wanted that someone to be Joy. I remember sending letters to Joy's home back in Detroit, just trying to see how she was doing, letting her know that I missed her and wanted to talk and clear the air between us. I would get ignored and get nothing in return. I didn't know what to think, whether she was really done with me or if she was still hurt about the things she heard. I still kept trying. I sent newspaper clippings to her home to let her know how good I was doing because she was always one of my biggest supporters, and I wanted her to see that I was coming into my own. Her mom and grandmother always had a soft spot for me, so they would read them and let her know I was trying to get in touch with her, but again, nothing. Maybe a year later, after I finally gave up trying to reach her, I got a call from my sister. She said, "Somebody wants to talk to you," and I said, "okay put them on the phone." My family would always call with people on the phone to allow me to talk to them because it had been years since I last spoke to them. She put this mystery person on the phone. When I heard this voice say "Hello," my heart instantly started beating fast because I knew the voice and it caught me off guard. Joy had stopped by my mother's house in Detroit one day while my sister, Kiyette, was getting ready for her high school senior prom and I guess at some point my sister told her how much I missed her and wanted to talk to her. I tried to play it off cool as if I wasn't about to jump out of my skin, and I told her to call me and stay in touch.

From that point on, I knew I had a chance of getting my high school sweetheart back. I knew that if I could just talk to her and let her know how much I missed her and wanted to be with her, she would accept me back in her life.

I always looked her up on "Myspace" to see what was new with her, and I saw that she had a baby. That hurt me bad because I wanted us to start a family together one day. I wanted to marry her and have our first child together just like we talked about in high school. I was only twenty-one years old with no children and was willing to accept her daughter as my own. We started talking heavy, like we used to in high school and I was trying to persuade her to come down to Indiana to live with me and that I could take care of her and her daughter. I had no idea how I was going to do that since I had just enough money to get me through school but I was going to make it happen somehow. I went to see her when I came home to Detroit to visit family. She was a dance/cheerleader coach, and I went to watch her girls perform. I saw some of the coaches who used to coach her when she was younger, and they were excited to see me and asked why I was in town. I told them that I was coming to get my girl and that I was taking her back with me. They said, "Well, go ahead and get her; there isn't anything here anyway."

I had just moved into a new apartment and had one of the rooms decorated with Dora stuff to surprise her daughter. I put up borders around the room; I had the matching toddler bed with sheet sets, borders, and stickers for her to see. I didn't know what I was doing but it was so much fun trying to figure out how to get those things to stick on the wall. And although she wouldn't know what anything was (because she was only a-year-old at the time), I wanted them to feel welcomed when they came. Joy finally gave in after months of my convincing and came down around September 2007. I was getting a lot of grief from family, saying that I was too young to take care of someone else's child and that it was a big mistake, considering how well I was doing, and I needed to stay focused on school and football. What they didn't realize was that this was going to help me focus even more because I wouldn't have to worry about trying to entertain a lot of girls.

Women can be a distraction, so just settling down and having someone with me would keep me in check. I was a very mature twenty-one-year-old and was ready to take the next step in my life. I wasn't like most of the guys who wanted to party and hang out every chance they got.

I wanted more out of my life. I was ready and willing to take on whatever responsibility necessary to be back with her. Being the oldest of five and helping my mother raise my little brothers, who are five, ten, and fifteen years younger than me, had given me a little experience with making bottles, changing diapers, and pampering babies. That experience for me was good. I left early in the mornings to go to class, practice and study hall, and when I came home, dinner was made, and I knew that this was what I wanted. Instead of going to get fast food or eating ramen noodles every day, I now had a girlfriend who would have home-cooked meals for me when I came home. I was comforted when I came home after a loss, and things were going well. We had a few rough nights in the beginning, when the baby would cry so loud and as I laid in bed and thought to myself, *this isn't going to work; I have to get up too early*. We somehow managed to get her on a schedule and they began adjusting to their new lives in Bloomington. I made sure to treat her as if she was mine. I would take her on walks with me, feed her, bathe her, change her; she was my daughter in my eyes, and I wouldn't treat her any differently. She treated me no differently either. She took to me like she had known me all of her little life. While my life was changing I made sure to stay on top of my grades and continued to do well on the field. I had to prove to my family that they were wrong and I could handle all the things I had going on in my life. Nothing was going to stop me from reaching my goals.

Life was good, and it came time to meet Purdue for the last game of that season. Not only were they our rivals, but we needed to beat them in order to make a Bowl Game that year. It was a fight for the "Old Oaken Bucket" in 2007. We fought a long hard battle with our rivals and it looked like we had a good chance to go to a Bowl Game, but we needed this win. It had been fourteen years since the Hoosiers' last made it to a Bowl Game. It was now fourth quarter with thirty-five seconds left on the clock with the game tied at 24. Every one of us had did all we could up until the point where we were. We had the ball, and it was fourth down.

The field goal was forty-nine yards away, and we all were standing to our feet as close to being on the field as possible. The anticipation in that moment was so overwhelming because everything was riding on our kicker, Austin Starr, making this field goal.

The ball was snapped, great hold, the kick was up, silence all around, everyone holding their breath; It's Good! We all started hugging one another and Mrs. Hep, who was there on the sideline with us even though she had lost her husband earlier that year, she wanted this win just as bad as we did. We owed it to our late coach, his wife, Indiana University, all the alumni that came through there and ourselves. With thirty seconds left on the clock, we still had to kick the ball off and get a stop, so the game wasn't over yet. In football, thirty seconds is a long time to go down the field to score a field goal or even a touchdown. What made it so hard, was that there were no more timeouts left for either team so all we needed to do was to get a couple stops inbounds and let the clock run out. We kicked the ball off, and our coverage team ran down and got the stop. They ran a play, we got a stop inbounds, and that was it; the clock ran out.

All of the fans ran onto the field to celebrate with us and lifted us up in the air, which was something I had never experienced. To be able to celebrate with everyone in the crowd, to win and bring the bucket back to our school, and to cash in on a promise that Coach Hep made, which was to play 13—it was now time, and we were Bowl eligible. It felt as if we had just won the Super Bowl. The excitement and the buzz around the media was so surreal. We felt like this was a turning point for the program, and it all started with Coach Hep restoring hope to the program. The Walk, the Rock, his excitement, his involvement in the community—it had all of our fans excited to see change.

Although he wasn't there with us physically to see his goals come true, we knew he was there with us in spirit. There were always doubters saying we were the same old IU and wouldn't make it to a Bowl Game, but we proved everyone wrong. We now had our chance to play in one. We were now waiting around in the locker room, watching TV to see what Bowl Game we were going to play in, and that was like the night before Christmas to see what gifts we got to open. We were all so excited and couldn't wait to hear the announcement. The results finally came in, and we were selected to go to the Insight Bowl in Tempe, Arizona. This was all new to us but we were ready for it.

The Bowl Week experience was top-of-the-line and was so much fun. We got new jogging suits with the bowl logo on them, an Xbox 360, a lot of per diem, and other small gifts. I always heard about different Bowl gifts that players get for going to a Bowl Game but never had a chance to experience it until now. We flew down to Arizona and had a pretty relaxed schedule outside of practice and meetings, so we had a lot of time to explore the city, spend time with our families, and enjoy our week in a new state. The committee that ran everything, made us feel very welcomed with their hospitality and service. We were so relaxed, and it felt so much like a vacation that it didn't even seem like we were there to play a game.

But now the game was finally here. My high school coach, Ken Fenton, was the only family I had at the game. He took me under his wing when I was in high school and had always been there. We started off pretty bad in the game and went down early to Oklahoma State. We made some plays and got back in the game. I don't think we were all the way in it because we were capable of playing better than we played. We drove down the field and I was so anxious to get a touchdown to say that I scored in a Bowl Game. We were about five yards out and ran a pass play. I had a swing route from the backfield, and Kellen Lewis our QB threw me the ball. I jumped over a guy near the goal line, dove in, and took a hard hit in my back as I was coming down and got in for the score. We made a comeback in the fourth quarter and closed the gap, but it was too late for us to come back for the win, and we lost by sixteen points.

We didn't get the result we wanted in the end, which was to win, but we came a long way from winning three games a season ago and we accomplished a lot, including making sure that we played 13 for Coach Hep and the entire fan base of Indiana University. We formed a bond as teammates that we will forever remember and we became a part of something special. We ended that year on a high, and I was now getting ready to go into my senior and final year of camp and college football and begin to step into the reality of life.

Sideline Reflections

"Years ago I was asked, 'Which is better: winning or competing?'

My response was instantaneous:

>'Competing. Because it lasts longer.'"

- Pete Carroll, Coach of the Seattle Seahawks.

Imagine how different my life would have been if I hadn't been so persistent with Joy?

Imagine how different my life would have been if I had stepped back once I found out that Joy already had a baby?

Every day, you find yourself at a crossroads. The conditions may be unfavorable. The odds may be against you.

Will you play the hand you've been dealt? Will you compete? Or will you fold? Surely, everyone would understand if you folded.

The question is - what future might you be leaving behind in the wake of your decision?

List a decision in your past, where conditions were unfavorable but you boldly pressed forward and won. What made you go against all odds? What would your life be like if you hadn't?

_____

_____

_____

_____

11

TWO MINUTE WARNING

Going into my senior year was a real struggle and a bit crazy. While I was in camp, working hard preparing for my last season as a Hoosier, I didn't have enough money to pay the light bill because I hadn't received my financial aid check yet, so our lights and electricity were out at the apartment and we had no hot water. I would sneak out my hotel where we were staying some nights and sneak them in the stadium to get a hot shower. Joy, her daughter, my younger brother, and his girlfriend were all staying at the apartment while I was in the hotel for camp. I didn't know what to do at that point for lights because I hadn't managed my money well enough to hold me over, so they were in the dark. They came up with the idea of running some extension cords out of our apartment door, down the stairs, and into an outlet that was for the building just to use the electricity for the microwave to heat up food. That was working for a while until neighbors reported that they were practically stealing electricity. Joy told me that we got an eviction notice and were being put out as a result of it. I couldn't understand why they were evicting us because I paid the rent on time, but it was because of the cords going through the hallway. I don't believe we even got a warning. As I was breaking camp, we had to find a place to stay and had to do it fast because we were about to be out on the streets soon. I was almost in the same exact scenario I was in a year prior.

At this point, things began to escalate and Joy and I were arguing to the point where Joy was ready to leave me. I was so upset and frustrated that I couldn't get through to her. I felt like I was being tested because I had been planning to propose to her on the same day that she almost walked out of the house on me and left for good. I had gotten the ring previously and was waiting for the right moment to pop the question.

I had my childhood friend, there with me to help me set everything up. I made up my mind to go through with my plan, and I had him set up a picnic blanket with balloons, food and slow jams playing on the speaker. Even though she was mad at me, I had a surprise for her and nothing was going to spoil it. We had talked earlier that year about being baptized so as one of the surprises, I set us up an appointment at our church to be baptized together that day. It was truly amazing to share that experience with her. At this point, she definitely did not expect a proposal after all the fighting we had just gone through. Though she was still a little upset, she went along with all I asked her to do. After the baptism, I blindfolded her, guided her down the stairs into the car, and drove around the parking lot of our apartment complex a few times to make her think we were going somewhere further.

The whole time I was thinking, *I'm really about to do this; I'm going to make my high school dream come true. I don't know what my future holds, but we will get through it together.* All right, I'm ready...pull yourself together. I finally parked and took her to the picnic area. As we got closer to the picnic blanket, I knew she could hear the music playing, and I finally took the blindfold off and we sat down and ate. She started to cool off and was wondering what was going on. After a bit I gave her a card that said "To my wife." She giggled a little bit and I asked her what was funny. She replied, "It's because it says 'to my wife'!" Bam—that was just what I was waiting for her to say so that I could ask

her the big question. I got up on my knee and said, "That's because

I want you to be my wife." I then proceeded to ask her to marry me and she just stood there, in shock, covering her face. Meanwhile, I was dripping with sweat, seconds away from passing out from anxiety but somehow also patiently waiting to hear her say, "Yes." She said yes, and I put the ring on her finger. We both were shaking. Meanwhile, my friend was taking pictures. That day, June 20, 2008, we will never forget.

As I began my senior year, I found myself planning our wedding, preparing to graduate and hoping to make it to the NFL.

During all this, Joy and I found out we were expecting our first child together.

That summer I spent most of my time training hard and putting things into perspective. I was so excited to finally have a baby that Joy and I shared together, and I prayed it was a boy. Three months later, Joy woke up in the middle of the night, screaming and crying in agonizing pain. She rushed to the bathroom, and we discovered she was having a miscarriage. I had to be calm for her and console her, so I had to hold in all of my emotions and be there for her. We drove to the hospital and the doctors kept her in order to determine what had happened. I had practice so I had to leave her but came back and checked on her as soon as I was free. She was in good spirits but we couldn't believe we had just gone through that. Within the next week, I received a call that changed my entire life. A friend back home called and told me that there was a possibility that I had a daughter and that I needed to come home as soon as possible to take a DNA test to see if I was her father. It was my spring break week, and instead of going to Vegas with my boys, I had to go home and see if I had a child. I went home for that week, and everyone was at my house waiting on my arrival to see me and my reaction after seeing her. Everyone there was certain, "You can't deny this one, y'all genes are too strong, she has to be your daughter." She was three years old, about to turn four that month. I didn't know what to think. I was shocked, confused, scared, and nervous. I always told Joy how we were supposed to have our first child together, but she had Jayla, and now here I am, I had a child before she did. I was so upset because I didn't know about her until she was almost four years old and missed out on all the baby years. I would have wanted to be there to see her grow. I couldn't get that time back if she was mine. All of these things were going through my mind, and at one point I just sat and looked at her in amazement, shock, and disbelief that this was happening. Joy sat next to me and asked me how I felt, and I couldn't describe it in words. I said, "This feels like a movie; I feel like I'm dreaming." She came running to me as soon as she saw me and called me "Daddy." That scared me. I knew there was a strong possibility that she was mine, and that had me just step back a little bit. I didn't know what this meant for me and my career or for me and school. I didn't want this to affect my schooling or my chance to go to the NFL.

I went and took the test, and when the results came back, they said that I was 99.9999% the father. I had my answer. We went to court to settle everything so I would be able to have rights as her father to see her, and I got joint custody. I was able to get my daughter, Diamond, for summer breaks and holidays, so when it was my time with her, she would come down to Indiana with me. We now had two little girls who were two years apart that we were taking care of and we were engaged. Our responsibilities quadrupled! After finding out, I was happy to know that I had a baby, and I wanted to make up for all the lost time. So we took tons of pictures and spent a lot of one-on-one time together every time she was with me. However, because of my schedule, Joy had both the girls a lot by herself until I was free.

This year had been full of so many ups and downs, and I don't know how I got through some of them, but I did. My last season of college football was coming to a close, and I fought my way through the entire year. My parents came to, at the most, four games that year because we didn't have a reliable car to get them there and we didn't have money for plane tickets. My family would watch as many televised games as they could, and if they didn't watch them, I would tell them how they went. It killed them not to be able to make it weekly but things were hard with trying to pay bills and take care of five children.

We only won three games my senior year and, at this point, I was so tired of losing. I've been on losing teams my whole life, and I knew that this could hurt my chances at the draft because we didn't get a lot of publicity. One moment that I will never forget is when my mom and dad came down for my senior game, which was my last game at home. I walked out on the field with my teammates, and we gave our Mother's roses and were able to stand on the field and hug them and let them be honored by all of our fans. I thought that was the coolest thing, to be able to let them see where we came from and to allow them to experience getting applause from all those people that supported us over the years. It was a great experience for us all.

My last game was bittersweet. I went out for pregame warm-up and looked around at the stadium and took in every moment because I knew that this was my last game at home as a college athlete. I was ready for the next phase but I wanted to have a great game and come out healthy.

The pregame speech that day made me really think; the coach was saying that this would be our last time playing together there. For some people, this would be one of their last games ever. Some would move on to the next level but majority won't. Putting things in perspective made me want to go out there and leave my mark and enjoy every minute of it. We went out, but we couldn't get anything going and got blown out. We went from a Bowl Game season a year earlier to only winning three games my senior year, which made all of the players coming out look bad and not worthy of the next level.

I started off with an agent whom I thought was going to get me to the NFL with no problem because the year before, he got two of my teammates drafted in the second round. I, for sure, wanted to be in that position, so I signed with him and went to his home to meet him and his wife. He had a very beautiful house. I saw glimpses of what I wanted in a home when I went there and knew that this was the right move for me. But a week later, I stopped receiving calls from him; he wouldn't respond to my texts, and I didn't know what to do.

The NFL draft was approaching, and I wanted to do some training to get ready for my pro day because I didn't get invited to the combine. I asked around about a new agent because I had to make a move to get things in motion.

I don't know how this came about, but I had a friend named Jestun on Facebook who wrote me and asked if I was all set on an agent because he had a guy. I said, "I do, but I'm about to fire him because he isn't doing anything for me and I haven't heard from him." He then called me with an agent on the phone, and we were discussing my pro day and how I needed training, and he offered to let me stay at his place and train with his people to get ready for my day. I had a good feeling from the first conversation that he was going to be good for me. His slogan was "Keepin' It Real," and he will tell it to you straight and will never beat around the bush. That's what I was used to, and I definitely needed that. He then went on to tell me that I needed to write a letter and send it certified to my agent. He said that he would help me with it, and he did just that. We sent the letter over, and he eventually faxed over a letter for me to sign to be with him, and since then, our relationship has grown. He has been my agent now for seven years and has gotten me to where I am now.

With my last college game behind me, a new agent on deck, two daughters, and a wife to be, I was hopeful about my future. It seemed like everything I ever wanted was all coming to fruition. There was only one more thing left to do at IU: walk across the stage. This was a pivotal point in my life. I graduated with a bachelor in December 2008 and finished second in school history with 2,009 career kick return yards, third with 4,658 career all-purpose yards, and tied for eighth with 21 career touchdowns. I became the first player in school history with over 1,000 rushing yards (1,621), receiving yards (1,028) and kickoff return yards (2,009), and I became the nineteenth rusher in school history to cross the 1,500-yard rushing barrier. I'm just the fifth player in Indiana lore to go over 4,500 career all-purpose yards; finished ninth in Big Ten history with 2,009 kick return yards; tied for third with 3 kick return scores; and shared sixth with 81 kickoff returns. It felt fake, like I was dreaming. Coming from Detroit—this doesn't happen to people like us. I was so happy. I accomplished something that hadn't been done in my family and was an example for my younger siblings and people from my neighborhood.

Not long after graduation, Joy and I found out she was pregnant with a boy. I was on cloud nine and prayed that this time we would have a healthy, full pregnancy. A month before the draft, Joy and I decided that we were going to get married before our son came. We were already doing things out of order, and we knew better. So we tried to right our wrongs and pushed our wedding date up, even though we conceived before marriage. We went to Vegas and got married at the Little White Chapel, and it was just us. We decided to have a bigger wedding when we made enough money to do so. That was all we could afford at the time and we wanted to make it official. It wasn't your storybook wedding, but to me, I loved every minute of it. I loved seeing my wife get dressed up in her all-white dress with her baby bump and all. She was seven months pregnant with my junior, and it took my breath away to see her walk down the aisle and to know that she would be mine forever.

Upon arriving home, time seemed to be moving so fast. Soon the 2009 NFL draft was just a couple days away. My mom and family planned a big draft party for me back home a few days before the actual draft. It was expected that I'd get drafted around the fifth or so round, so there was so much excitement in my hood, in my family, and around the city about the party and the idea that a kid who grew up in a place like Detroit could make it to the league. So many people came out to celebrate with me— childhood friends whom I didn't even know still followed me, or looked up to me, for that matter, were all in attendance and all very encouraging. I couldn't believe this was all for me. La'Crecia crossed my mind so many times because I knew she'd be in attendance too if she were still here. But all of this was dedicated to her, her memory; all that she never got the chance to do. I even heard that her mother was going to try to come. I don't know if she ever made it or not but that night was one to remember. After the party, lots of pictures, and a few drinks, Joy and I headed to downtown Detroit to stay at the MotorCity Casino Hotel, where my auntie Tawanna was able to get us a room to allow us to get away from all the distractions and await the call.

The day of the draft, we sat in the room and my agent called and told me not to watch the draft the first day because it would only frustrate me to see all the players getting drafted and my name not being called. So the second day rolled around when the sixth- and seventh-round picks were named. That morning, I woke up bright and early from a rough night's sleep because of the anticipation. I reminisced about how I used to watch the draft when I was a little boy, envisioning them calling out "and so and so selects Marcus Thigpen" and listening to the crowd applaud so loudly that it made my heart tremble. This was the day I'd dreamed about for as long as I could remember, and the suspense of waiting was killing me. As I waited anxiously to hear my name being called, the seventh-round picks began, and they started naming their picks. And I waited and waited…

Sideline Reflections

Imagine: Being a star football player but struggling to pay your electricity and water bills.

Imagine: Lining up the perfect proposal only to almost fail by an unplanned argument.

Imagine: Facing eviction because someone else was stealing electricity in your apartment.

Have you ever been so close to success but felt so far?

In the book "Think and Grow Rich," author Napoleon Hill tells the story of R. U. Darby.

Darby's uncle had gold fever, so he staked his claim and started digging. After a lot of hard work, the uncle found a vein of gold! He covered up his find, and returned home to raise the money for the machinery that he would need to bring the gold ore to the surface. Darby soon traveled with his uncle back to the site after raising funds to make their fortune.

Things started well and before long, they had enough to clear their debts. They were excited, everything from here on would be profit and things were looking good. Then the supply of gold stopped. The vein of gold ore had disappeared. They kept on digging, but found nothing. After a while, they quit in frustration and sold their machinery to a junk man for a few hundred dollars. The astute junk man called in a mining engineer who checked the mine and calculated that there was a vein of gold just three feet from where Darby and his uncle had stopped digging.

Whenever you feel like giving up, remember that you may be just three feet from gold.

Do you remember a situation where you were so close to quitting but stuck it out and "reached your goal?

_____

_____

12
TIME OUT

The anticipation ached in the pit of my stomach like hunger pangs. I waited and grew more impatient with every name announced. The final draft call was coming, and, wait….It wasn't me, I wasn't in there, I didn't receive a call from anybody. "What didn't I do right?" I began to ask myself. I didn't smoke, I didn't drink, my grades were good, my Pro Day went great. I mean, I was one of the fastest guys there. I ran a 4.29 in the forty-yard dash, but maybe even that wasn't enough. Yeah, I was on the smaller end, but I was stronger than most of the guys who were called. I began to question my worth, my training, my grind, my dream.

I was promised a seventh-round pick, and though that wasn't ideal, just being drafted, period, was good enough. My pride took a big hit, harder than any hit I've ever taken on the field. To say I was shocked is an understatement. I was hurt. I felt like I let everyone down. I let myself down; my dream had just gone down the drain. What will I do next? I didn't have a plan B; I had a degree but didn't know what I would do with it, it was just a piece of paper. This can't be the end; I didn't come this far for it to end like this. I sat there looking at the television in disbelief. I felt like I was dreaming or that perhaps there was still another round of drafts. How did they miss me? I started contemplating on what I would do next. How would I make money now for my wife, two girls, and a son on the way?

I didn't have too much work experience. I didn't know where I was going to stay, and as a married man with kids, I didn't want to be a burden on family and ask to stay with someone when I was used to being on my own for the last four years taking care of my responsibilities. I had to clear my mind, so I walked down to the fitness center in the hotel, sat on the bench, knocked out a few sets with tears in my eyes and then I walked into the hallway. I looked at my phone and I had two voice mails. I had one from my agent and another from a number I didn't know. I was anxious to see what my agent had to say but I wanted to know what this other number was that I didn't recognize. Was this the call that I was waiting for? I listened to both voice mails, and then I called my agent back to see what he had to say. When I spoke to him, he asked me if I heard anything, and I told him I didn't get a live call but I did get a voice mail. The voice mail was from the New York Giants, and they were calling to sign me as a free agent and wanted to bring me in but I missed the call. When I told my agent that, he got very upset because he'd told me to make sure my phone was on and charged as I could receive a call. I could have possibly missed my opportunity to play in the NFL. He explained how serious this process of free agent signings was, and that they go very fast, so hopefully they would call back. I waited another five minutes, and my phone rang again.

"Hello, is this Marcus Thigpen?"

"Yes sir."

"Marcus, this is Brian from the Philadelphia Eagles; how would you like to be a part of our team?"

I said, "I would be honored to be a part of the team."

They went on to say, "Marcus, this isn't guaranteed, you will have to come in and prove yourself and earn a spot on the team. We want to bring you in as a receiver and as a returner to compete with our guys who are already here." As I hung up the phone with a smile on my face, I was excited to be going there to get my journey started as an Eagle. I hadn't been a full-time receiver, but in my mind, I was an all-around athlete and I knew how to catch the rock. The scout told me that he would send me my flight itinerary and all I needed for off season minicamp.

Before we ended the call, he told me what to expect. At that moment, tears dropped from my eyes because of all the frustration of being undrafted, wanting it so badly, and working so hard for it to not happen. It was still a privilege to get my foot in the door, and I was beyond grateful for the opportunity no matter how small my chances were. I'd been wanting to be part of the NFL my whole life. I've always admired players like Barry Sanders and Herman Moore, being a young Lions fan, and now I finally had my chance to prove myself as an NFL player like these guys.

I went up to the room and told Joy the news; she was very excited. She hugged and congratulated me. I felt a sense of peace getting that call. We then went to my mom's house and my brothers and sister were there. They saw the news with the rest of my family as it scrolled across the bottom of the television on ESPN, saying that Philly signed me as a free agent. As my family began to cry tears of joy and relief, it took everything in me to hold back my tears. All my boys that I grew up with on the block, my Fenmore family, every dude I played with from little league with the Panthers, to my Mumford Mustangs—in that moment, everyone was happy to share a piece of this joy with me.

Later that night, I went back to the hotel as I awaited the e-mail from the Eagles with a detailed agenda. I was at a point where I thought, *OK, I made it*, and although I didn't know what to expect, I thought I at least should finally receive some nice paychecks to take care of my whole family. I got all my details for the flight and started packing my things. I had to leave behind my pregnant wife and daughter Jayla. My other daughter, Diamond, was living with her mother for the school year, so I would see her when I came back home. It was tough leaving them behind. I wanted to be there to be able to help my wife through her labor pains and the weird food cravings that she had. I had to leave in order to be sure I could provide for my growing family. We both had family in Detroit, being that we were from there. I couldn't fathom asking someone if my family could live with them while I went away to pursue my dream or even ask for money for the things my wife and kids needed. We had food stamps, but that couldn't buy clothes for our daughters or diapers when our son was born. I let my pride get the best of me, but I knew I had to do something before I left. An aunt I had met only a year earlier offered to let Joy and the kids stay with her until I could get on my feet and make the team.

We had a great support system that was always there for us and always helped us out. Whenever we were down and out and couldn't find a penny, someone always gave us a hand. I packed up the little bit we had and helped move my eight-months-pregnant wife and Jayla into my aunt's home, kissed them good-bye, and flew out that night.

End of Second Quarter: Coaching Points

You don't get character because you're successful; you build character because of the hardships you face.

—Herman Edwards

We often dream of success and what we want to be in life and get discouraged when things don't work out the way we visualized it. Never give up on your goals and dreams and the visions that are instilled in you. Just because it doesn't happen when you want it to, doesn't mean it won't happen. Keep knocking, get back up, keep fighting and never give up. The door will eventually open, and when it does, make sure you are prepared to run through it one hundred miles per hour.

Sideline Reflections

In the book "The Obstacle is the Way," author, Ryan Holiday shares the phrase "ruthless pragmatism." The ability to turn negative situations into positive ones... or at least to extract good fortune from misfortune, to snatch whatever benefit we can, from these negative situations. Having the right perspective, separating oneself emotionally from what has happened, is the key to being able to take even negative situations and applying positive action to them.

What situation held you back in the past where you responded by practicing harder, finding weak spots, recruiting allies, seeking mentors, or turned an obstacle into an opportunity?

_____

_____

HALFTIME

The entire flight there, I couldn't sleep. I was anxious to show everyone in Philly what I was capable of, but at the same time, this was the first time I had to leave my wife not knowing when I would return. I closed my eyes and exhaled slowly and focused on the positives, determined to make a way. I must've dozed off because before I knew it, I felt the turbulence of that plane landing and the wheels touching down, and I smiled. Getting off of the plane, the first thing I saw was a guy with an Eagles shirt on holding a sign with my name on it. I never had this type of treatment and even though I was a free agent, I was treated like a draft pick. I got my bags and went down to the hotel where they had all the players, and met my roommate. This phase was minicamp and off-season workouts to see what we had. I got to sign my first NFL contract, and I took a few selfies with my cell phone to send to my wife and mother with tears coming down my face. Although it wasn't guaranteed, my dream was now within reach.

That day we learned plays, met the coaching staff, and learned our way around the facility. The itinerary we had reminded me of college but a lot shorter because it wasn't the real deal yet. We got up at 6:30 a.m. and had to be downstairs for the shuttle buses to come and get us to take us to the facility. Seeing the Eagles logo stamped all throughout the facility—on the doors as I walked in, on the carpet, and all over the walls—it reminded me of all the work I'd put in up until that point. I was in awe but kept my cool and had to act like I'd been there before, but on the inside, I was smiling ear to ear. We walked in as the new rookies on campus to take physicals and get fitted for our cleats and helmets. It was like the first day of college all over again. We had a brief team meeting shortly afterward and broke up into individual meetings by position to install the first phase of our playbook. I'm glad I had practice doing this in college because I wasn't too overwhelmed. A lot of the concepts were the same just different names and a few different routes. I've never had a problem learning plays because I knew if I wanted to play, I had to know what I was doing when I was out there.

My way of learning the plays faster was by making my playbook on Madden, the football video game, and running them continuously. I would look at the play that I had on paper, draw my routes up on the game, and run them against the computer until I knew them. That helped me out a lot and allowed me to speed up the learning process because I made what would be boring to most—just looking at paper—fun and interactive by doing something I loved and learning at the same time.

This was my first time being a full-time receiver, so I had to make sure I knew how to run routes, get open, and catch the ball. I came in the next day thinking I was going to be faster than everybody, like I had been my whole life, but at this level everybody was fast. There were guys who were three hundred pounds moving, and I was shocked to see guys that big running the way they were. Being out there with guys I once watched on TV but now was on the same team with—I couldn't believe it. Catching balls from Donovan McNabb, going up against Asante Samuel, and learning plays from Deshawn Jackson . . . it didn't get much better than that. I was in the same rookie class as LeSean McCoy and Jeremy Maclin, and we all hung out and were really cool. We were learning the ropes together; they were drafted and I was a free agent, but we were in it together. The weight lifting and running program that was in place wasn't hard compared to college because the strength staff didn't think it was necessary to go through the extremely hard two-hour workouts. Everything we did was short and sweet. Workouts were intense but no more than an hour, and we didn't have people all in our faces yelling to get one more rep or trying to burn us out. They were smart about taking care of our bodies, as opposed to college where it was like they didn't care and had us so sore we could barely walk after workouts.

We started at 7:00 a.m. daily and would be done at or around 1:30 p.m. It seemed like we would have meeting after meeting after meeting. Then we would lift and eventually get on the field to run the plays that we'd met about. We met so much because we had to know all the plays, hand signals, and the checks and audibles inside out. When it was time to scrimmage and play opponents, we had to be very detailed and know exactly what was going on. We had weekends off and we would often link up, just the rookies, and go bowling or something. On May 21, I had to go home because my wife was going into labor. I didn't want to miss it because I had already missed my daughter's birth; I didn't want to miss my son's. My aunt called me with an update on my wife. She had already purchased me a plane ticket because she knew I couldn't afford it as I was trying to make the team, but I had practice that day and couldn't leave until later. By the time I got home, my JR was born.

I couldn't believe I missed another one. I was there shortly after but I didn't get a chance to see the whole process. It was my first time seeing my baby from birth and I was ecstatic holding him in my hands. He was so small and I didn't want to drop him. I couldn't do anything but stare at him in amazement thinking that we created this life. Meanwhile, my wife was talking to me and falling asleep every ten seconds. The doctors had her drugged up, so she was out of it. I now had a new why and more motivation. I could only stay that night; I had to fly back out and it would be a few more weeks before I could come home for a bit. I wanted to let my wife rest and recover while I was there, so I held our son the whole night in the hospital with her while she recovered.

I got back to Philly and continued doing my thing on the field, in the weight room, and in the meeting rooms. I felt good leaving there, leaving a good impression and excitement with the coaches until we came back for the real deal. I was still one of the fastest guys but I was also still one of the smallest guys, if not the smallest.

I never let that affect me, though, because I could go blow for blow with anyone, no matter what size they were . We are all grown, and I could hold my own. I've seen and been through it all in Detroit, so none of that phased me. I wasn't at all intimidated.

The rest of minicamp went well, and I was able to go back home to Detroit for two months before I had to be back for training camp. I was so happy to be able to spend some time back home with my wife and kids, who were still staying with my aunt. I was able to see my mom and siblings as well as some of my high school friends. But as much as I loved my city, I was ready to move and start a new chapter. I wanted more. I wanted to move away from the cold and to a cleaner, safer environment. We would always hear gun shots at night, and Joy would always tell me that we needed to get out of there because she didn't feel safe, and we had babies to protect. I was already thinking it but we didn't have the finances to get up and go, though I was trying my best to get what we needed so we could move. That was an added pressure for me because although I was living my dream, at times it would be hard to focus in meetings when I knew my wife and kids were at home and didn't want to be there, and I couldn't be there to protect them. I had to lock in and focus, but some days it was hard because I wanted to be home with my newborn and spend time with my wife. We didn't have a honeymoon, and we were apart more than we were together, almost as if we were in a long-distance relationship. It was hurting me and my wife on the inside because we were newlyweds and couldn't enjoy one another. We had to figure out how to make things work regardless of our circumstances. For me, I saw what she didn't see because she was stuck in the house with the kids, and we were struggling.

The funds that I was bringing in from minicamp weren't getting it done. My vision was moving into a nice home, having a nice, reliable truck, and being able to take care of our own needs. My whole mind-set was that I had to make it because I had so many people depending on me. My family, my friends, my enemies—I had to show everyone that my potential far exceeded what they thought they saw in me, and I knew I could persevere at this level. The critics would say things like, "He's too small," "He can't catch," "He can't take the big hits." I was never known for getting hurt and would play through anything, so I didn't know where they were getting their information from. I had so much on my plate, so much pressure on my back to make the team. I didn't have a plan B. My plan B was to make plan A work at all costs.

I went to training camp with the Eagles, and those had to be the longest days I've ever faced. I thought college was hard, but when I got to training camp, this broke me down to my knees every night. I wanted to quit and just go home but my purpose was way bigger than me. I wasn't just doing this for myself, I had two daughters and a son who shared my name now, and if I stopped, who was going to take care of my family? Leaving a legacy was my new goal, not just making it there. Camp was tough, though, and designed to challenge my mind-set and my abilities. The thing that broke me down in camp was waking up at 5:45 a.m. to eat breakfast and going straight to meetings until 8:00 a.m. Right after meetings, we had to get dressed and go to the field and get ready for practice. I would be in full pads out there, banging with my teammates like we weren't teammates. I was thinking, We were just cool in minicamp; now you're trying to take me out? Then I realized that we were really competing for jobs.

HAMILTON TIGER-CATS
Football Administration

Hamilton Tiger-Cats | Tel: 905.547.2287
1 Jarvis St. • Hamilton, ON | Fax: 905.549.6610
L8R 3J2 | www.ticats.ca

April 28, 2011

To: All Players

Welcome to the Hamilton Tiger-Cats. Below are the equipment guidelines for the 2011 training camp. Please read all of the information, as the organization maintains strict equipment guidelines. My staff and I look forward to assisting you throughout training camp and appreciate your compliance with the information provided.

Responsibilities of the Athletes:
- ✓ **Shoes**: including turf, grass and gymnasium.
- ✓ **Gloves**
- ✓ **Long sleeve black shirts** – required for early morning practice and only colour accepted during season.

Please note: These items **will not be supplied** by the organization for the duration of training camp.

It is strongly advised that you keep a lock on your locker at all times during training camp; therefore you will need to bring a lock with you as one will not be provided by the team.

Responsibilities of the Hamilton Tiger-Cats:
- ✓ **Laundry Bag**, including socks, jock and team t-shirt.
  - The laundry bag remains the property of the Hamilton Tiger-Cats
  - Laundry provided cannot be altered
  - The cost of altered laundry will be the responsibility of the athlete, i.e. cutting t-shirts

Please do not hesitate to contact me directly if you have any questions regarding the equipment guidelines. My staff and I look forward to meeting you and wish you the best of luck during the Hamilton Tiger-Cats' 2011 Training Camp.

Sincerely,

Drew Strohschein
Equipment Manager

It's like being in your field of expertise and you have to come in with the best reports, have the most calls made or make the most sales. But for us, we had to make plays. I understood that this was their way of living and surviving. I was sixth on the depth chart and was fighting and clawing, trying to crack me a spot on the roster.

We all went from practice to get straight into the cold tub, which was a pool full of ice, to recover and get ready for the next practice. After three hours of running and banging, we had lunch at 11:00 a.m. We had a little break and had to be back to meetings at 2:00 p.m. to watch the practice that we just finished, go over more plays, and continue learning the play-book and perfecting it. After meetings we had to get a lift in that was short and sweet because we had another full-padded practice. Instead of going back to the hotel, I would usually sleep in the locker room without even taking a shower because I was so tired and needed rest immediately. To me, that time went so fast; it seemed like as soon as I closed my eyes it was time to get up and we were right back on the field like we never left. After we got done with practice, we had dinner from 6:00 p.m. until 7:00 p.m. Right after dinner we had night meetings, which would last until 9:30 or 10:00 p.m. When I got to my room each night, all I wanted to do was sleep. Training camp will break even the toughest athlete down. It was almost 11:00 p.m. before I finally got in and I had to be right back up in six hours to do it all over again. It was the day in and day out grueling process that separated good from great and, honestly, some nights I just wanted to go back home to my family. My mentality took a beating that made me rethink everything. I had to do some readjusting.

U.S. TRACK & FIELD AND CROSS COUNTRY COACHES ASSOCIATION

Marcus Thigpen
Indiana University

is hereby recognized as a member of the

2007 NCAA Division I Outdoor Track & Field

ALL MIDEAST REGION TEAM

4x100 Relay

Big Ten Conference

This Certificate Is Presented To

Marcus Thigpen

Of The

Indiana University

In Honor of Being Named

Men's Outdoor Track & Field Athlete of the Week

March 31, 2008
Date

Commissioner

Indiana University

School of Continuing Studies

To all who may read these letters, Greeting:
hereby it is certified that upon the recommendation of the Faculty,
the Trustees of Indiana University have conferred upon

Marcus Arnette Thigpen

the degree of

Bachelor of General Studies

in recognition of the fulfillment of the requirements for this degree.
In Witness Whereof, this diploma is given at
Bloomington, Indiana, December 20, 2008.

The Board of Education
of the City of Detroit, Michigan

Samuel C. Mumford High School

this

Diploma

is awarded to

Marcus Thigpen

who has satisfactorily completed the requirements for graduation prescribed
for the Public High Schools of the City of Detroit,
June 11, 2004

MARCUS THIGPEN #34
Miami Dolphins RB

RESIST & PERSIST

3RD QUARTER

THE DREAM

13

ADJUSTMENTS

I would often reminisce about being nine years old, lazy, never wanting to go to practice. I thought natural ability was good enough, and practice wasn't necessary for me. But my mom would drag me out of the house and we would walk thirty minutes down Pembroke Avenue to the Panthers practice field. On those days, I could hear her telling me, "If you start something, you better finish it." Conversely, I would hear my wife in my head, telling me, "You got it, baby, keep going, we got this here under control, you just do what you gotta do to make your dream come true." It was this type of support that wouldn't let me quit even when I wanted to. Believe me, there were times when I wanted to but I had to do this for them. Some nights, after fighting the sun for hours on the field, running play after play, fighting the next man for the same spot and fighting the negative thoughts in my mind, I cried to myself, battling internally because so many depended on me. My mental game was being tested but I knew I had to push through. My wife was doing her part; let me do mine—let me stop feeling sorry for myself and go out there and get what's mine. My mind was made up and I decided to give it my all.

A couple of weeks went by, and as we were nearing our first preseason game, the coach called me into the office and instructed me to bring my playbook. My first thought was that I was about to get involved more because of the plays I had been making at practice. As I grabbed my backpack and headed over to the office, the closer I got, the more my heart raced. "Marcus, have a seat." I sat down and looked him square in the eye, anticipating what he had to say next. He began to tell me how well I was performing in camp thus far and how I'd done everything expected of me. I can't tell you how relieved those words made me feel! Then he took a deep breath and just as I thought my place was secure, he hit me with, "But . . . unfortunately, we're going to have to let you go. It's a numbers game, and though we'd love to keep you here, we can't find a roster spot for you right now." As we closed out the meeting, and he thanked me for my time, I zoned out. I was seven years old again being struck by that car. I walked blindly into a line of fire that I didn't even see coming. I did everything they asked me to do, just like I did what my uncle asked me that day. I left my family, I missed a birth, I sacrificed the most important things in my life for this opportunity. To be told none of that was enough shattered me. His mouth was moving, but I heard no words. My emotional auto-pilot kicked in, and I thanked him for the ride, the experience, and for their consideration. My flight home was booked. I felt worthless and didn't know what was next for me or how I would begin to tell my family.

I quickly called my agent, Rob, to see if I had any other options or if this was the end. He's a God-fearing man and very optimistic, he encouraged me not to lose hope and reassured me that he was going to do what was necessary to get me another shot. Rob had been through this before and had clients in this situation, but this was my first time and I had no idea what was about to happen. I couldn't comprehend it. I put my heart into this, my blood, my sweat, my tears. I gave this my all. I was up at 4:00 a.m., running in the streets of Detroit—running with a knife in my hand because it wasn't the safest place to run, but I had to get my cardio in. I put the work in that was required. Why didn't it work? That same night I made it back home to my aunt's house, where I was welcomed with hugs and a nice dinner, I couldn't even eat. I had to release some tension and clear my mind, so I went up to Mumford High School, ran, and worked out. I kept telling myself that I wouldn't be denied like this again.

I got a call a week later to be with another team, and we were so excited as a family to get another opportunity. I flew out to Denver to be with the Broncos, and this time they wanted me to be a running back and a returner. I was a running back my whole life, so this was great news to me. Being a receiver helped me out a lot because my routes were way better than any other back. And now I was a two-positional player on top of being a returner, which added more value to me as a player. I came into training camp late, so they were way ahead of me, and just like being in a college course, missing numerous days, weeks, even months, it's hard to be proficient when you're trying to play catch-up.

The first night after practice, I was back in my room coughing up blood and having nosebleeds, and I had no idea why. The next day in practice, I was barely breathing. I couldn't understand why it was so hard for me to catch my breath until I finally realized that we were in the mile-high city, and the altitude there was a significant factor. I was worried that I was getting sick, so I went in and told the trainers what was going on. They said that it was normal and that my body would adjust to it, and it would eventually stop. I felt a little more at ease but was still concerned. The practices were a lot easier here, and they took care of our bodies better than they did when I was in Philly. The second practice on our two-a-days were usually helmets only, and that took a lot of stress off the body.

I was picking up the plays quickly and started to nail down the blocking assignments, but my downfall was that I was small, weighed about 190 pounds, and was tasked with protecting the quarterback from guys who were 250 pounds running at him full speed. That said, it was my job to pick up any blitzer, and while I was at a considerable disadvantage, I stood there and took on all comers. Sometimes I made the block, and other times I got knocked on my butt. I was always the smallest, but my heart, my drive, and my will kept me above the rest.

Things were looking good for me. I told my wife to fly down, because once camp broke, we'd need a place to stay, and I wanted her to come down and help me pick it out. My wife and my son came down, and we looked and found some beautiful places, but none that we could afford on the little workout bonus checks we were getting. We found an apartment that we knew was the one, and I had just enough to put down a deposit to hold it in hopes of making the team.

Later on that week, we had an away game. I'd flown many times before but; this time was different. It was a chartered plane with "all you can eat" food, drinks, movies and every imaginable type of game. Being from the "D" and knowing a little about gambling, I had to get in on the tonk and spades card games being played so that I could take some money from them. Private flights have different rules! No one had to sit down with seat belts fastened and tray tables up. None of those commercial flight rules applied here. These perks were the crumbs from the table of the "good life," and the Broncos knew how to live the "good life." We landed in Seattle and made it to the hotel where the security was tight, with cops on all of our floors to make sure no guests came up. We were well protected.

"Top of the world, Ma!" The kid from the "D" was about to play in his first NFL preseason game against the Seattle Seahawks! As I walked onto the field for warm-ups, staring at the crowd and stadium, I felt like I had finally made it. Although I had only been there for two weeks, being a Bronco seemed like a good fit for me; it felt like a dream. Seeing the NFL logo painted on the field and the lime and navy Seahawks name printed in both end zones was surreal. It was an unforgettable experience!

As the ball was kicked off, I stood on the sideline, waiting and waiting for my turn. As the quarters rolled by, we were down. Our returner muffed a punt, and I thought it was my time to get in the game. But, he was drafted and projected to do great things, and it's my belief they kept him in to redeem himself, so I continued to wait. My moment to shine would come in the fourth quarter where I was able to get a piece of my first NFL action. There were about two minutes left in the game, and on my first play, I got the ball and ran up the middle for about two yards before I took my first NFL hit. Man, it felt good to get that first carry. At that point, I could say that I did at least get one carry. Next play, I got the ball again and ran up the middle, didn't see anything, and then bounced out to the outside for a gain of twelve yards before I got knocked out of bounds. I looked back, and there was a flag on the play; it was an offensive hold. After that I was called back out of the game; on the sideline, I got a few high fives and "good run" compliments, and that was it for me.

We lost the game, but I finished with two carries, one of which didn't count because of the penalty. We got to the locker room and the head coach was telling us what went wrong, what adjustments we needed to make before the next game and how we were going to go about doing it. Although we lost, I was all smiles because the experience alone to carry the rock at the NFL level gave me a different perspective and a renewed confidence after being released from Philly. I remember calling my wife after the game and she told me she had fallen asleep. She said when she saw I wasn't in all game, she started dozing off. I had to fill her in on what happened on my two plays because that was a pivotal moment for me and she missed it. She could hear the excitement in my voice but she didn't know whether to congratulate me or feel sorry for our loss. Even so, nothing could steal my joy that day.

We flew back the same night and had meetings the next morning to watch the game and make some corrections. As we watched film, my coach was impressed with what I did with the little that I had. I took advantage of my opportunity and got what I could while I was out there. It wasn't what I wanted or what I had liked but that was the nature of the business. I wasn't there that long and didn't know everything, so I didn't expect to get a heavy load but I sure didn't think I was only going to get two plays near the end of the game. As we broke meetings, I was walking to my locker to check my cell phone before the next session, and the scout came and grabbed me and told me the coach wanted to see me. I had only been there for two weeks; my plays were positive and practices were going great. I was killing it in the weight room, surely they weren't about to cut me. But this was the same guy who brought me in, so maybe they just needed me to fill out more paperwork.

I got to the office and, sure enough, I met with the general manager and the head coach. It was the same song and dance it was in Philly. They told me, "We love your work ethic, your commitment, you did everything we asked, you made plays for us. But we have to shape up our fifty-three-man roster and we tried finding a spot for you, but it's a numbers game and we can't find a way to keep you right now. We have to let you go—but stay in shape because we could be calling you back here in a couple of weeks. We'll help with your flight arrangements to get you home." And it hit me all over again. The "what if's," the "why's and how's" all came crashing down. Once again, I had to tell my wife to pack up, we had to go back home. The deposit we put down on the apartment was all that I had to my name. Thankfully, the leasing office was kind enough to refund it to me. I walked away that day without a shred of pride, an ego at an all-time low, and a $750 cashier's check.

Sideline Reflections

"The green reed, which bends in the wind, is stronger than the mighty oak, which breaks in a storm." - Confucius.

After going all out for the Philadelphia Eagles, playing a new position, I was unceremoniously CUT. I had missed the birth of my child - only to be CUT from the team before playing a single game. Staying focused earned me a tryout spot on the Denver Broncos - and my first NFL game! But despite my performance - I was CUT again.

Rejection is one of the things we, as human beings, fear the most. It always feels personal (despite what they say). It never feels fair and it always feels like the end of the world. But being able to find a way to keep going, after such a personal rejection, is one of the few traits ultra-successful people have in common.

A young Walt Disney was rejected for lacking imagination.

The Beatles were rejected by several record labels before they made it big. A few years ago, J.K. Rowling shared her cringe-worthy rejection letters with fans. Among other things, she was told to go back to writing school. The manuscript for Harry Potter was rejected countless times, before one publisher finally took a chance on her.

Life has lots of rejections lined up, ready and waiting for you.

It also has rewards beyond your imagination at the end of all those rejections.

But how do you find the self-esteem, willpower and grit to push through rejection after rejection?

What are some very painful rejections from your past that you recall?

How will you push through rejections that are coming in the future… on your way to success?

_____

_____

_____

14

FLAG: DELAY OF GAME

After being cut twice, I almost became numb to it. It still stung, but this time around, my emotions shut down. As we packed our things, I could tell my wife sensed my frustration. She looked at me and said, "Stay positive." She said it was their loss and that I'd be back somewhere soon. "Keep going and don't give up just yet." None of this made any sense to me as I began to dissect my skills and my worth, not thinking about the business side of the sport. I was just as strong, just as fast, and made plays like everybody else. I knew it was harder for a free agent to make the team but I couldn't figure out what more I needed to do to make it. I had to make some decisions because I knew waiting around wasn't going to get me anywhere. My godmother, Rhonda, lived in California, where she worked at a group home. She offered to let us stay with her, so I decided to move there with my wife, daughter, and son. She welcomed us with open arms. The main reason I wanted to leave was that I needed a change of scenery and had to change things up to get different results. Rhonda told me that with my degree in behavioral science, I would be a good fit for the kids.

We flew out to Cali, and it was such a beautiful place we thought about making that home. The mountains off the highway, all the hills, and the weather was beautiful. The traffic and the people, however, weren't the nicest. The four of us slept in one bed in one of the rooms that they allowed us to use. We had to make it work, and they made us feel very comfortable in our transition. My godmother had been trying to get us out to Cali for the longest time because it was such a better life for us than Detroit. I took all the steps necessary to get the group home job, and at this point, I was content with where I was. I had a job that allowed me to help out with bills while also being able to provide for my family. The goal was to save enough money to get our place. Some of the kids at the group home were there because their parents were in jail or deceased, while others were placed for behavioral issues. I wanted to be a role model to these young men and give them all I had. When they would talk about their experiences, I felt and saw the pain they were facing. I did all I could to keep them on the right track and encouraged them to stay positive. They loved that I played football and wanted me to keep pursuing my dream, and their fire for the game inspired me to do just that.

Shortly after I began working at the group home, I hooked up with a trainer named Ron. One of Ron's clients, the Labon's, a beautiful couple whose close marriage and happily blended family we greatly admired. I would talk to them about my family and my NFL goals and the challenges of balancing the two. I talked about my wife and kids so much; it was as if they knew them, though they had never met. They pushed, encouraged, and inspired me not just to be a better athlete but more importantly to be a better husband and father as well. God always placed people in my life who wouldn't allow me to give up or become complacent.

Between working out and working at the group home, I barely saw my family. I was working from 2:00 p.m. to 10:00 p.m., and that was the whole day. When I got home, it was time for bed, and I would do the same thing all over again the next day. Saturdays and Sundays I would work from 6:00 a.m. to 10:00 p.m., and I wouldn't see them all day, but at the same time, I had to do what I had to do as a father to provide. We found out that we had another baby on the way, and I had to put in extra hours. Those extra hours came through as we were able to get our own place a few months later. It felt amazing to be able to provide a roof over my family's head myself.

A week after moving in and getting settled, I received a phone call. Joy was in a bad car accident and the driver at fault ran her into the side of a building. If that wasn't bad enough, she was pregnant.

I was worried about her, concerned about the baby, and my mind kept going back to the crash. I got my kids into the car and raced to the hospital. To my relief, Joy was all right; she hit her stomach on the wheel during the impact, but she and the baby were perfectly fine. That same day, my agent called me and told me that he had an offer for me to go and play in the Canadian Football League (CFL), but I would be on the practice roster as it was late in the year. Being on the practice roster would work out well as it would provide a fair chance of making the active roster the following year. I talked it over with my wife, and she was okay with it because she wanted me to keep pursuing my dream. She knew I loved football and that this would be a great opportunity for me to get some film and be able to one day get back into the NFL.

The downfall was, I'd only be making $500 a week after taxes which was less than what I was making there. I took the offer and had to leave my family behind again—and it wasn't just a quick flight away. It was a different culture and a different country.

I went and began to learn the differences between American and Canadian football—things such as three downs instead of four, the CFL field was 110 yards long and 65 yards wide, compared to the NFL standard of 100 yards long and 53 yards wide. They could motion going toward the ball calling it the "waggle," and in the NFL you can't. They also had to be a yard off the ball on the defensive line, whereas in the NFL, you could be just a few inches away. Regarding my position as a returner, they had a five-yard halo rule where you couldn't be within five yards of the returner, and in the NFL, you could be right in the player's face. They also played twelve on twelve instead of eleven on eleven. I started out in Regina, Saskatchewan, a place that I had never heard of but I have to say, the Roughriders were pretty good; they were one of the better teams. They'd made a few Grey Cup appearances the previous years and had one of the best fan bases in the CFL.

The plays weren't too hard to learn, and the practices were way easier than in the NFL. They had a four-hour rule, where we had to meet, practice, and lift all within that time frame each day because they couldn't afford to pay us beyond that, unlike the NFL. My pay was the same regardless because I was just a practice body trying to earn my way onto the active roster. I was having great practices and showed a lot of promise for my future. I came in confidently because I had NFL experience and knew if I could play at that level, then I should be able to play in the CFL. I was still in great shape because I never stopped training. I was sent home prior to the playoffs and they went to the grey cup that year and lost to the Montreal Alouettes. After a missed field, they had a chance to re-kick because too many players were on the field for us. They made the next one and we lost by one point.

Once I returned home to California, I was back working at Murrell's Group Home, offering all the wisdom I could to help steer the kids down the right path. We tried moving my mom and brothers out to the west coast to give them a chance at a better life. But, as the saying goes, "home is where the heart is" and their hearts said "Detroit" all day long.

Time was flying and I was getting ready to leave again for off-season workouts in April with minicamp and pre-season following right after off-season workouts. The season starts earlier and ends earlier in Canada because it gets so cold toward the end. So as I went back, I knew I had to make a statement. I was considered a rookie and had to attend rookie camp with a few other guys. So, I went in and killed rookie minicamp. I was the best rookie out there, and the coaches knew it as well. I got a lot of compliments, and I knew I was making the team this year; there was no way I wasn't.

I played in the first two pre-season games and had significant returns. I was the leading rusher for our team. We had cuts coming up soon, but I wasn't worried at all because my performance spoke for itself. One day, after practice I was called to a meeting with the general manager. He told me that I'd had a great training camp, great rookie camp, and great pre-season games. I said, "Thank you, and I look forward to having a great season as well." He then went on to tell me that they could only keep so many Americans and so many Canadians because of the ratio. I said I understood, and he then went on to say that they had reached their maximum number of Americans for the team; I thought, surely I was a part of that figure. He said, if someone got hurt or if they had an opening, they would certainly call me back.

An opening? I didn't make it again? How is it possible I didn't make this team if my stats are number one? I looked him in the eye and said, "Thank you for the opportunity," and left.. I walked through the locker room and all my teammates were shocked when I told them the news. They didn't understand how it was possible for them to have cut me. The words of my teammates, "Don't worry, Thig; you will be back somewhere soon," echoed in my ears as I made that long, bitter trek home, again. We were only about a week away from what would've been my first CFL game.

Having been cut as many times as I had should have crushed me. In fact, most people would've given up, gotten angry, threw in the towel, or taken it out on everyone else while letting their dreams slip right out of their fingers. But I'm different, I've always been different in the sense that things never really got the best of me. I stayed neutral, never got too low or too high. I knew the value of my craft and expected to exceed in whatever I did, so when it didn't happen, I was like, "okay, life doesn't stop here; on to the next." I always knew another opportunity would come, and it was just a matter of time. Coming from Detroit and from a family who had nothing, I've been let down a lot but I could visualize this happening for me and didn't let my current situation dictate my future.

Many times in life we have setbacks that deter our pride. One of the main things that I've learned through the process is that it could always be worse. We may suffer significant personal loss but, whatever challenges arise, we must learn to face them and not let them defeat us. In football, when you get a flag for delay of game, it's usually because you are either unaware of how much time you have on the clock, or you're trying to make adjustments because you see something in front of you that wasn't part of the plan you prepared for. It's okay to take a moment to step back and reorder some things because life will always throw something at you, but our hope for the future and the possibilities that lie ahead are endless. I had to remind myself that even the greats failed before they succeeded.

> "I've missed more than 9,000 shots in my career. I've lost almost 300 games. Twenty-six times, I've been trusted to take the game-winning shot and missed. I've failed over and over and over again in my life. And that is why I succeed."
>
> —Michael Jordan

Sideline Reflections

> "Our actions may be impeded, but there can be no impeding our intentions, or dispositions because we can accommodate, and adapt. The mind adapts the obstacle to its own purposes. The impediment to action, increases action. The obstacle to the path, becomes the path."
>
> -- Marcus Aurelius, the Last of the 5 Good Emperors of Rome.
> (Emperor from 161 to 180 AD)

In the book "The Obstacle is the Way," author, Ryan Holiday shares how Marcus Aurelius, known as the last of the 5 Good Emperors of Rome, learned to thrive not just in spite of obstacles, but how to actually thrive BECAUSE OF obstacles.

Perception is how we see and understand what occurs around us, and what we decide those events will mean. While we can't change what has actually happened, we can control how we perceive it and respond to it. Our perceptions can be a source of strength, or one of great weakness.

How can you practice:

Being objective and not subjective? _____

_____

Keeping an even keel? _____

_____

Finding the good even in discouraging situations? _____

_____

Steadying your nerves, when others would panic? _____

_____

Ignoring what disturbs or limits others? _____

_____

Focusing only on what can be controlled? _____

_____

15

EXTRA POINT

In my pursuit of success, I was hungry. While waiting for my flight back home to my family, I searched for motivational videos, read inspiring quotes, and prayed for anything that would push me beyond my current limits. I came across a video on YouTube that changed my life. In this video, this speaker kept talking about a guru who would help this guy attain the keys to success if he met him at the beach at 4:00 a.m. The guru referenced wanting to succeed as badly as you want to breathe. The passion that I heard in this guy's voice was authentic, and when I noticed the D on his hat, knowing he was from where I was from made him that much more relatable. Eric Thomas's video called, *How Bad Do You Wanna Breathe*, sparked my will to keep going because I felt like I was at the end of my career. I had been cut three times and thought maybe I was done with ball; that maybe I saw something in myself that others didn't see. Maybe I think I'm better than I really am. Like breathing, succeeding in football wasn't an option but a must! I was going to do whatever it took. I listened to ET's video repeatedly and regained sight of my worth after wanting to call it quits.

When I made it home, my wife had been in the hospital for a week because she was having a lot of complications with the pregnancy. Though I was released, it was a blessing for me to be home because I wanted to be there for her to make sure she was well and support her and keep the kids while she rested. After missing my first two babies' births, I really didn't want to miss this one. These were moments I could never get back. Joy was six weeks away from her due date, but the doctors could not stop her contractions, so they decided to deliver the baby—ironically, the day I flew in. It was like my baby was waiting for me to get home and when I did, it was time for her to come out. While we were preparing for the surgery, my agent called and told me that a team wanted to sign me right away. I had only been back for a day and had another offer from Canada. However, I refused to miss this moment, so I told him, "I'll have to leave after we have our baby."

My wife gave birth to our daughter Mariya on June 24, 2010. Watching my daughter come into the world was one of the happiest moments of my life. She was beautiful and I couldn't believe God loved me enough in that moment to give me something so amazing after all the things I had done in my life. I cut the cord, held her little body in my arms, with the biggest smile on my face. Just as we got settled back in the room, my agent called again and told me when my flight was, and I had to go. This was a few hours after the birth. It broke my heart to have to tell Joy I had to leave again, but I knew she'd understand. She had her mother in town to help her out, thankfully, so I knew she had the help she needed.

I had another opportunity to go and play. I was told I would be the starting returner on opening day. I came in, signed the contract and got my jersey. I was number 33. I didn't really like the number, so I went to the equipment manager and asked what else he had. He had the number 8, and that was it. The number 8 meant a new beginning, and for me, this was exactly that. I took that number and said, "I have to make my mark on this one."

When Joy was finally released from the hospital, she came home to a note on the door stating that we had thirty days to get our stuff out of the apartment or the sheriff was going to come and put our things out. It always seemed like it was one struggle after another. As I prepared to learn a new team and a new playbook, I had to figure out where my wife and kids and brand new baby would go. The Labon's offered to let my family stay with them until we could find another place to stay. My trainer, Ron, and the Labon's helped Joy move all of our things out and into their place.

It was a very humbling situation for me as a man to have to depend on people I just met to take care of my family while I was away. But I'm forever grateful for their sacrifices for me and my wife and kids. As they got situated, I could finally focus on my job with the Tiger Cats.

They wanted me to be the primary punt and kick returner and to also play receiver and running back, and I was all for it. I never caught a punt a day in my life, but I wasn't about to turn down this contract, so I told them, "I can do it all." I knew I could learn on the fly. I had two practices before the game and I was thrown right in the fire, but I was ready. I had been out of football for a while, but I was itching to get back out there. We had an away game and I barely knew my teammates but, what I did know was, I was tired of being told "No, you're not good enough." On game day, during my pregame warm-up, I saw a few guys on the opposing team whom I had played with in Saskatchewan. We were all released around the same time in Saskatchewan, and a few of us ended up on other teams. They were just as shocked as I was that I was let go, and they told me to take it easy on them. It was crazy how some people saw my potential, but others didn't. I knew what I had in the tank, but the coaches didn't. We came out, and they sang their national anthem. That's when I realized I was no longer in the United States. It wasn't the U.S. national anthem but it still sent chills through my body.

We won the toss and received the opening kick. I caught the ball near the left numbers, went up straight, cut to the right middle, and there wasn't anyone there. I ran through as fast as I could. I saw the kicker and jumped over him as he dove, went back down the left sideline, and scored on the opening kickoff. My first time touching the ball was a touchdown. The coaches were happy, and my teammates came and jumped on me until I fell to the ground. I was so hyped and determined to show everybody what they passed up on, and this was only the beginning. Later on that game, they tried kicking a long field goal and I was back deep in case they missed it. I was going to return it. The kick was up and wide to my right and I thought, okay, I got a shot. There are a lot of big guys out here, let me set it up, slow play it, and hit it on them. I caught it, ran up the field to set up a few guys, cut to my left, took it straight up the middle for 119 yards, and got the touchdown.

My first game playing and returning, I got two touchdowns but I still wasn't satisfied. I was hungry for more. I wanted to show everybody that I belonged in the NFL. This was the game that allowed me to showcase my talent at the pro level. I had never had two in one game on returns, and I was shocked myself. I knew I had the ability to do great things but had never had the opportunity. After the game, I had all the cameras and microphones in my face, trying to figure out how this happened and where this came from. It was a great outing but we didn't win, so I couldn't enjoy it the way I wanted to. I had been praying for a breakthrough and it was on the way. The income there was better than anything that I'd ever seen. We were making about $60k before taxes within a six-month time frame, and for a student fresh out college, that wasn't bad. Little did I know I wouldn't even see half of that. After Canadian taxes were taken out, it was down to half, and then trying to exchange Canadian dollars to U.S. dollars, I lost even more.

Sideline Reflections

"A ship is safest at the shore. But that is not what it's there for."

- Albert Einstein.

I had been cut three times in a row now. But finding a new mentor in Eric Thomas - took my determination to another level. And just in time, too, because during this period, I also had to deal with flying right back out after my baby's birth for a football gig, and leaving my family facing an eviction notice!

When I got the offer from the Canadian Football League, I realized that persistence really does pay off!

Many might have expected me to look down on the CFL opportunity.

But Heraclitus, a Greek philosopher of the late 6th century BCE, said this: "Whoever cannot seek the unforeseen sees nothing for the known way is an impasse."

Many centuries later, George Washington, the first President of the United States, and Commander-in-Chief of the Continental Army during the American Revolutionary War, would cite a similar sentiment while waging war against the British Army: "Never attack where the enemy expects."

I took all the rejection, found an opening along the flanks, and jumped all over the small opportunity. As you'll find out, that small opportunity in the Canadian Football League would soon lead to other things.

It turns out that most wars are not won by great armies going head-to-head in a frontal attack. Most wars were won by attacking from the flank, by drawing the opponent out of their defenses, by applying nontraditional approaches, or by using psychological advantages.

Think of a particular path to your goal that has continuously been blocked. Can you think of a nontraditional approach? How can you approach your goal from the flanks?

_____

_____

_____

16

MOVING THE CHAINS

It was such a struggle for my wife to be by herself with the kids while I was away, so we decided to move to Texas to be closer to her relatives in Dallas. Moving now seemed to be the norm for us. We were in a new place or new state every couple of months, it seemed like. With all the moving costs, a bigger family, and having to pay for housing in both Canada and Texas, at the end of my first year, I didn't have much money left. I've always managed money pretty well but I just didn't make enough to support the weight of all of the responsibilities we had. This was why making it to the NFL had to happen; I couldn't survive like this. But this was the process, and I was fully invested.

I usually had to report for camp in April, and the season didn't end until December. It hurt me to have to leave my wife and kids behind for eight months at a time because I wanted to be there for them and watch them grow. I missed everything—birthdays, first steps, first words . . . I missed my wife. We would Skype every break I had so that I could see the kids and feel like I was still a part of their everyday routines. They were my daily motivation to keep going day in and day out.

As the season in Hamilton went on, I was getting more and more attention, and there were talks about me leaving and going back to the NFL. That was my goal, but I was in a two-year contract and had to stick it out one more year. With all the talk of me leaving the CFL, I was concentrating on staying healthy and playing one game at a time, continuously getting better. I'll never forget our quarterback, Kevin Glenn, who was from Detroit as well. He was older, but we connected right away. He taught me a lot about the game, and having someone from your city, your hood, on the same team is rare. We connected on a lot of different levels, more than just ball. We called our weight room in Hamilton "the dungeon." It smelled like sweat, and the worn-down, old-school feel of it reminded me of Detroit. When we had days off, I would be the only one in there, working with my iPod on, still listening to my old Al Green. I would be the only one on the field running stadium stairs and sprints after practices. I had to get back to the NFL, and the only way I knew how was by outworking the next guy. I wasn't the biggest, and I wasn't the fastest, but my work ethic spoke for itself. I wasn't about to be outworked by anyone. It helped with my soreness from the games as well. I was able to run off some aches and pain and get my body ready for the next game. KG, our quarterback, threw me my first receiving touchdown at our next home game. That was my first receiving touchdown, but my most memorable moment from that game was when I took a punt return from my own thirteen-yard line, shook off a defender, juked a guy, and took off up the middle. I had only the kicker to beat. I went left, came back right, and went back left, and he fell right in front of me. I didn't expect that to happen, so I leaped over him like I was running hurdles and had no one else to beat. I saw a guy coming up on me as I was looking at the big screen, and he dove and swiped at my ankles. I jumped over his hands and went in and scored. I made the Top 10 plays of the week on ESPN back home, off of that play. None of that was planned; it was all instinct, and hearing the home crowd go nuts had me so hyped. I had a two-score game on the road, but to come home and do it in front of our fans who supported me made it that much sweeter. At this point, I was on pace to set a CFL record, which was to be the first player to score five different ways. I had no clue this was even a record. I had a missed field goal return, receiving, kick return, and punt return, and now all I needed was a rushing touchdown.

We got the opportunity to play against the Saskatchewan Roughriders, the team that cut me, and I was out for blood this game. I was angry, holding a grudge, pissed off at them because they let me go.

The coach's first words when he saw me were, "We screwed up, huh?" I just smiled, but on the inside I was feeling some type of way about them. This was toward the end of the year, and I needed to get that rushing touchdown—and what better team to make history on than this one?

I was playing wide receiver the whole game, and our running back got tired, so I was next up. We were in the red zone, going in for the score about five yards out. Coach called a run. This is it right here my first year in this league, and I'm about to make history. All I had to do was get five yards and they were already a yard off the ball. I was in the backfield, sizing everybody up and seeing where I had to go and making a plan in my head. Set hut, the ball was snapped. I got the rock, went to my right, and saw the linebacker there. I only needed a few yards; I had to give it all I had. He grabbed my legs as I dove forward with the ball. I reached out, straining to cross that white line because I had no idea if I would have another shot this game. I went down, looked over to the right and saw the referee running in with both hands up, signaling a touchdown. That was it; the record was broken at home in front of my own crowd against a team that doubted me. It could not have happened at a better time.

My first year was a blur and went by extremely fast. I had struggled so hard to make it to this point that I was almost in shock at the success; however, I always knew I was capable of this. I was nominated "CFL Rookie of the Year" in our conference.

Sideline Reflections

"You are either competing to be the best you can be, or you are not."

- Pete Carroll, Seattle Seahawks coach.

Many of us see our skills as static. We see ourselves as "good enough" and become complacent about getting better. It's human nature.

I refused to be satisfied, and it took me to the top of the Canadian Football League.

In her book "Mindset: The New Psychology of Success," psychology researcher, Dr. Carol S. Dweck, uncovers the differences between two core mindsets. The FIXED mindset and a GROWTH mindset. Through analysis of research, Dweck shares why the Growth mindset leads to a more successful and fulfilling life.

The Fixed Mindset leads most of us to believe that particular traits are naturally gifted, innate, and cannot be developed. When you hear "nature versus nurture" this is the "nature" argument. This leads to trouble with esteem and self-development in the face of mistakes and failures… because people accept that this is their lot in life. They can't get any better. The Growth Mindset, change is constant. People place an emphasis on learning from mistakes. Instead of placing permanent labels on themselves-like Fixed Mindset people do.

In the Growth Mindset, intelligence, creativity, athletic ability, can be developed with proper practice, hard work, endurance, and a willingness to learn and adapt. But in a Fixed Mindset, these abilities are fixed and cannot be improved.

What if Michael Jordan had a fixed mindset and decided, after being relegated to the Junior Varsity team, to quit basketball or to not aspire beyond mediocrity?

In what areas have you been stuck in a Fixed Mindset? How can you embrace failure as growth?

_____

_____

17

TOUCHDOWN

With all the accolades, touchdowns, and broken records, I still didn't bring home enough money to make ends meet until the next season, so when I got home to Texas, I had to find another job while trying to get a gym membership to work out and take care of my family and the bills we had. I had previously worked in a group home but I wanted something that was much less time-consuming than that. I did a little research and found a job where I could deliver phone books. The pay was okay and the hours were flexible. It was an extra something to hold me over until I got back to making more during the next season. Most people would look at this as bottom of the barrel, but I was glad to have the opportunity to earn some income and be home for the most part while doing it.

As I look back on it now, I'm glad I experienced the struggle and hardships that I did because it produces character in a person. It keeps you grounded and humbled—and I was for sure humbled by this experience. Here I was, a professional football player, but I was in my living room with my wife packing a thousand books into bags, driving around nice neighborhoods with humongous homes that were so beautiful, dropping off phone books at their front doors. I made it fun, though, and enjoyed it. I actually met some nice people. My wife helped out, and my sister-in-law, was the driver as we hopped in and out of the car from one house to the next. My little white Lumina was sagging in the back because of all the books in the trunk and in my backseat. Every time we hit a bump in the road, the back of the car would scrape the road. We would send the kids off to school and get straight to delivering the books. We had a certain time period to get all of the books out by, so we would just go and knock it out.

The whole time I was doing this, I was encouraging myself, saying, "It won't always be like this; I'll get that big house and that black Cadillac Escalade I just saw at that house." Instead of complaining every day, I went out there and stayed motivated. This part of my life was the turning point because I felt on the inside that there was more to life than this. I couldn't be a pro football player delivering phone books. I should be on a beach right now, relaxing with my family, enjoying some off time before I reported back, but I had to work to keep the lights on, clothes on my babies' backs, and food on the table to eat.

At this point, I had been with Philly, Denver, Saskatchewan, and now Hamilton. I was very grateful for these opportunities but my ultimate goal was to get back to the big stage in the United States in front of fans who sing the national anthem I'd heard my whole life. I felt like a traitor when I first heard the Canadian national anthem because it wasn't where I was born, it's not my country, I don't know any words from it—but it was still powerful.

I had a solid second season with the Tiger Cats, and my goal was to continue getting great film, stay healthy, and try to take my talents back south of the border. I was under a contract where I had signed a two-year deal with Hamilton and an option in which the option was theirs, and I couldn't leave and go to the NFL if they wanted me to stay because I had signed and would be fined if I didn't stay. The thing that helped me out was that the CFL had just put a new CBA (collective bargaining agreement) in place, which allowed me to opt out of my contract if I had a workout with an NFL team, and they signed me. I was free to go, and I was for sure leaving if the opportunity presented itself. But if it didn't, I knew I could go back to where I was. My agent, Rob, was letting me know about a few teams that wanted to bring me in for workouts, simply to run a forty-yard dash, do some drills, run routes and catch balls, and take physicals to make sure I was healthy. I felt butterflies in my stomach all over again because the opportunities were right in my face, and for more than one team to have interest in me gave me a sense of pride that I had finally proven myself. At the time, I didn't know anyone who had played in the CFL and went to the NFL and had a successful career. I don't know if it's because the game is different, the talent level, or what, but it is very rare that it happens.

I had been through three cuts already and I knew what was expected of me. I knew the maturity level I had to have and what it took to make it and stay at the NFL level. I studied plays and players, I watched countless hours of film, I ran and lifted like I never had before, and I was ready for my workouts.

First team up was the Miami Dolphins. I was flown in to this beautiful city that I had never seen before with palm trees and fancy cars everywhere. It was amazing. I was instantly sold just off the scenery alone. The organization was just being rebuilt with a new head coach, staff, and general manager. The first thing I did was take a physical to make sure I was able to perform and run and had no pre-existing injuries. I then went over to meet the head coach and see the facility. This facility, in comparison to Hamilton, was like rags to riches. I went in and killed the workout. My measurables were great. I caught every ball thrown my way, ran well, and was in great shape. I was there with a D lineman and a linebacker, and we were all individually working with a coach. I spoke to the general manager at the end, and he was telling me how much he had watched me and that he wanted me in there to compete for a job and help make the team better. He went on to tell me that he wanted to sign me to a three-year contract, and at that point, I was ready to take that opportunity right then and there and not go to any other workouts. I had more offers, but why leave what I had here? I was intrigued by his words and felt wanted, for a change. I was always at the tail end of things and had to scratch and claw to get what I wanted, literally working my way up from the bottom of depth charts to make a team.

I called my agent after the meeting and informed him that they wanted to sign me. He told me that we still had to weigh our options because there were other teams that could possibly offer a better deal, so I should keep my options open. "You put the time and work in, so now it's time to cash in on your investment," he instructed me. I was okay with what he said and trusted his judgment because he always kept it real and knew the business way better than I did. If it was up to me, I would've signed right there on the spot, though. I flew back home to Texas and kept preparing because I had another workout in a few days.

Next up was the Jacksonville Jaguars. I flew in, and things were different. The welcome wasn't the same, the treatment wasn't the same, and the scouting director I spoke to didn't know much about me. He didn't know I returned kicks and punts and thought I was only a receiver. I was already done with them because who would really invest in a product they know very little about? I just came from a team where I felt appreciated; I was known and was told what was expected of me and these folks didn't know me—I was ready to leave. But I took my physical there and put together another great workout. The general manager was out of town but the scouting director said he would be in touch. He said he liked what he saw but couldn't offer me anything at the time. I called and told my agent about this interaction, and he immediately got pissed because he felt it was a waste of time—as did I, but it was still an opportunity, which was good. In the meantime, the Dolphins were trying to put an expiration on their offer. They knew I had workouts with other teams and wanted to get me off the market before someone else gave a better deal. So they threatened to take the offer away if I didn't get back with them soon. Now I had a dilemma. Do I take this offer or go to the next workout? My agent always left the decisions in my hands but would give advice on the situation.

I had Houston next on my list, which was closer to home but how could I know if they would act like Jacksonville or not? What if they offered a better deal than Miami? If I missed out on this Miami offer and Houston didn't offer anything, what would be next? Should I keep going to workouts until I got another offer or just take this one?

I spoke to my wife, my boys, and my family and got advice from them. I prayed on it because I had to make a decision fast. They were telling me to take my talents to South Beach like LeBron did. They were already telling me something that I wanted to do anyway. I called my agent. "I'm going to take the offer in Miami and be a Dolphin. I prayed on it and had to seek out wise counsel, and this is my decision," I told him. He got on the phone with them, and it was set for me to go back down to Miami and sign the contract. I was flown back down to sign the papers to make it official and to see the facility and be shown the ropes. After I signed, I remembered Jeff Ireland, the general manager, telling me, "This is your workplace now; you have unlimited access to it and can do whatever you feel necessary to prepare for organized team activities and camp here." I had a couple of stints before this but this felt different. I felt like I was at the top of the pyramid and not at the bottom of the barrel this time.

I flew back home and when I got there, the kids had decorated the home for me with pictures they drew all over the walls, balloons, cookies they'd made for me to congratulate me. They sure did know how to make Daddy cry. I was so happy, and they were just enjoying the process, not knowing what I was going through so they could be happy. When they smile and when they're happy, it makes everything all worth it. At that moment, I knew I had to deliver. I knew I had to make it. I had no choice because I knew they depended on me. They had no idea what it meant for me to sign with a football team and what could happen for them and their future. They only knew that Mommy was happy, I was happy, and I'd be playing football. My whole mission was to give them everything I never had.

As hard as my mother worked, there were a lot of days, Christmases and birthday's when we had to go without because things were tight financially. The older I got, the more I understood struggle, and the less I needed those Jordan's. Let's pay this bill and get dinner for the night; I'll get those shoes another time. I was at that same point with my children, and I didn't want to repeat what I went through, so every day I was up at 4:00 a.m., outside jogging in the dark, in the cold, going to the gym three times a day. These thoughts went through my head; If my kids wanted Jordan's, I wanted to be able to get them. At that point we had to get shoes and clothes from Walmart or resale stores and be happy with it. It chewed me up on the inside when they would ask me for something and I had to come up with an excuse as to why they couldn't get it at that moment.

There was one point where I had thirty-five dollars to my name, and I had a check coming in a few days but I spent it on a pre-workout supplement. I knew that my body was my résumé, and once I whipped it into shape, got stronger and faster, I would be able to stand out when I reported to off-season workouts.

I had a fairly small signing bonus of $7,500, but that alone was bigger than three weeks' worth of playing in the CFL, so I was happy about it. We were able to get rid of our '93 Lumina and bought a used '05 Durango truck, and we were also able to get out of our apartment and get a new home, which my wife found that had more room for our growing family. Things were starting to move up, but they were moving slowly. I had a great off-season and never tried hiring a trainer because I couldn't afford it, and the things that they charged for were things I already knew how to do from experience. Some things you can't teach; they only come by experience of actually doing them, and I knew that.

It was time for me to leave my family once again to go to off-season workouts, and there were endless possibilities ahead of me. The Dolphins flew me down to Miami and put me in a hotel. I received my itinerary and saw that the schedule was a little different from what it was before. There was a new CBA in place in the NFL, and I wasn't a part of the league when there was a lockout. So when I came back, things were a lot easier. Days were shorter, and some rules had changed; for example, you can't have a certain amount of days in a row for practice—no more real two-a-days. All I had to do was show up and give all I got for a maximum of three hours, and the second practice was always a walk-through due to the rule change. We could only have so many padded practices as well.

I had trained hard in Texas, where the humidity was also high, trying to prepare myself for the heat I had to face in Miami. After my first day at practice in Miami, I realized this was a different kind of heat, just like the air had been a different type of air in Denver, and I couldn't prepare for it. I was struggling to breathe and started sweating as soon as I stepped on that field. I thought it was only me, but as I looked around at my teammates, I saw that some were being taken in to get IVs for dehydration. Others were overheating and had to lie down with ice on their heads just to keep from passing out.

As we were going through practice, I reverted back to when the general manager told me, "We have a third-round draft pick as our kick returner, and you have to come in and compete to earn a roster spot." I was on a mission and it wasn't anything personal against him, but I had to feed my family. I went out there with the intent to take his spot and whoever else was standing in my way. Every day I was getting better; arriving early, leaving late, doing extra work, trying to set myself apart.

In the meantime, I had family and friends back home congratulating me and wishing me well when I hadn't even made the team yet. Nobody really understood the process; they thought that once I signed my contract, I was locked in. Some family members would get mad at me when I told them I couldn't send them any money. A lot of people had their hands out, and I barely had one hundred dollars in my bank account. People saw dollar signs, but all I saw was four other dudes I had to beat out to make the team. From the outside looking in, you would think that when you sign a contract you're guaranteed that, when in fact nothing is guaranteed. Even when you sign a three-year deal, you could be cut at any moment. I knew that because I'd been there. They didn't. The checks we were getting for off-season workouts were just enough for me to pay rent back home and take care of clothes and food and the necessities.

We were coming to a break before training camp, and it was time for me to get home with my wife and kids and spend some time with them before I was gone for the season. As much as I wanted to be there and loved them, I wasn't planning on coming back until the season was over.

We were in sort of a distant relationship because I was always on the go, and we couldn't take everyone because our kids were in school. A lot of decisions were hard to make, but this was a once-in-a-lifetime opportunity. So when the door opened, I had to sprint through with no hesitation. This was life as we knew it. Skype calls were a must, texting all day while I was in and out of meetings was a must, and when I got home, falling asleep on the phone every night was how we got through.

I was home for a month before I had to head back. I had all my accountability partners (Nick, Sav, Kev, AB, Jay O, Preston, Rich, and C-Wheel) come down to do some training with me. During that time, I was rejuvenated, had some fun, got some great work in, and was ready to get back after it. That refresher was key for me.

Another thing I liked to do was go back to Detroit just to see the city, to see where I came from and where I didn't want to go back to, and that motivation carried me through the season.

Camp was here, and it was time for me to go and claim what was mine. These days were even warmer than before. There were days when it was 110 degrees out there, and our coach would take us in after a while to finish in the AC. I went there every day with the kill-or-be-killed mindset. Leading up to the first pre-season game, I was doing some great things. I was running a return to the opposite side of the field in practice, and as I opened up my stride to get going, I felt a tug in my hamstring and immediately throttled down and started jogging to a walk. My coach was yelling from the other side of the field, "Thiggy, let's go!" I walked over to the trainer to let him know what I felt. This can't be happening right now, not now. I'm on the brink of being the starter and this is a setback for me. I can't let this stop me. I tried getting back out there to do a few strides down the sideline and was limping, so they wrapped my leg up with ice. I was standing on the sideline, angry, looking at them grinding while I was standing there, looking soft. I never miss practices and would fight through injuries, but I couldn't this time.

Practice was over and we went in. They did a further examination to find out what was wrong. The results came back, and it was nothing serious. It was a sprained hamstring, which was good but the bad news was that I would have to be out for at least a week to let it heal with treatments four to five times a day. "A week? I can't sit out a week; my first pre-season game is in three days and I'm starting," I said to the head trainer.

His response was, "You're not starting this one because if you go out there and tear it, that can take you out for months, so you can miss this first game and come back next week for the second one. That's why they give us four pre-season games!" He laughed as he told me this. I wasn't laughing at all. I know how hard it is to make a team—I'd been cut three times and I was healthy, so being hurt would kill my chances. My special teams coach, Rizzi, came in and made sure I was all right and told me to get healthy because they need me back out there. I thought to myself, *they really like me here*, and that pushed me to get healthy faster. I was in extremely early every morning, rehabbing, strengthening my hamstring, and doing everything required. It hurt having to watch the first game on the sideline and not dressing, especially because the HBO show Hard Knocks was filming our entire training camp. I watched from afar, wishing I was out there.

I remember, at one point, I felt a huge calmness come over me as I stood there with so much anxiety. I started running the next week and was able to get back to full speed and practice with the team, doing everything, and I felt great. It was time for me to shine now.

We had an away game against the Carolina Panthers, and I came and got my spot back as the returner. We received the ball, and I was in my first-ever NFL game as a starter and playing as a returner and receiver. I was a little nervous, but not too much. I kept telling myself, "You're here now, no turning back. Let's get it!" That whistle blew; we all lined up, they kicked it off, and for a moment, I only saw lights flashing and heard the crowd roaring. The emotions I had going were crazy. I had butterflies, but calm ones. I caught the ball, ran up the middle, and tried jumping over two people. I gained about 35yds and had a solid return. I had to wait on the sideline until the starters got out for me to play offense, but I was doing all the returns, so I was happy about that. I knew I had to make a great impression, and I knew this was the way for me to make the team, so I had to leave all that I had on the field.

After the game, we flew back to Miami and had the next day off. The staff was starting to make roster cuts and had to get the roster down, so some people had to go. I'd been through this process before but this time was different. I actually had some film to evaluate and was given the opportunity to play more than two plays. When we got back, everybody wanted to go out and party, but I just wanted to talk on the phone to my wife and watch the game film to see how I did. I knew I was going to have to answer some questions as to why I made some of the decisions that I made, so I wanted to be prepared. Besides, I hadn't done enough to go out and party. I wasn't the partying type and I was on a mission to make the team and stay focused, and going out wasn't going to allow me to make the team.

I was feeling great after the game, with no aches or pains, but the next morning, my back, neck, arms, and legs were sore. I felt like I had been hit by a train. The adrenaline that I had from the night before had worn off, so the next day I felt all the hits that I had taken. On my off day, I stuck with my same routine that got me there. I went and got a workout in at the facility to get rid of my soreness and to get some blood flowing through my legs.

The next day in meetings, we went over the film, and as I was sitting in my seat in the team meeting room, I started looking around and noticed about seven or eight guys were not there. I knew the first round of cuts had come up and I was still there. I had made it through the first round. My first two stints in the NFL with Philly and Denver, I didn't get that far, so I was already ahead, and my confidence took a boost. I knew I still had a lot of work to do, being a free agent who had just come from the CFL. I had a lot to prove to the coaches, to the league, and if Miami didn't keep me, I had to do enough for another team to sign me. But my coaches were impressed with the game that I had. My return averages were top of the league that week, and I caught a few balls as receiver, too.

It was back to work as usual for the week and the next pre-season game, and I had to keep stringing good practices and games together. I got a taste of what it's like to play in an NFL game and was comfortable now. I was ready to keep it going. My film study increased, my attention to details increased, and I was understanding the game more. The next two games I had, I went out and had solid performances.

We were now at the last game of the pre-season, and the final roster cuts were coming up. The next two days were the most nerve-racking days that I have ever had. I was in my hotel room, staring at the phone. I had the TV off and was hoping to get a call to say I made the team. I laid down and took a nap, and while I was asleep, I remember dreaming of getting the call saying, "Congratulations, you have made the team, and you're a part of our (53) fifty-three-man roster." I woke up and there was still just silence from the phone, but I kept hearing the elevator, and I didn't know if people were just coming in or out or what was going on. I was new to this and had never been in this position before. I was used to walking into a meeting and getting pulled to the office to get my release papers.

The whole day I didn't get anything, and we had meetings the next day to game plan and get ready for the opener at Houston. When I heard the elevator beep the fifth time, I opened my door and saw a teammate with his bags packed. I asked him where he was going. He said, "They let me go," and we both shook our heads. We shook hands and wished each other the best of luck.

At that point I realized that I didn't need to get a call; in fact, I needed that silence because if you got the call, then the next noise to be heard was the elevator dinging. It's a tough reality; only one-percent of all athletes make it. After seeing that, I was hoping my phone didn't ring. Please don't ring, please don't ring. I was talking to my wife, and she was also praying that I didn't get a call because she knew how badly I wanted it and how hard I worked to get where I was.

To be at final cuts halfway through the day with no call had me on edge. I woke up in the morning and went to the facility, still not knowing how this whole process was supposed to work. I went in and saw that my locker was still there. I was eating breakfast, getting ready for meetings, and didn't see many people. We had our team meeting, and Coach Philbin congratulated us all on making the team and told us how it was a privilege to be sitting in those seats. There had been a lot of tough decisions made, and he told us that he had to make a couple more moves, but for the most part, this was the team. "Oh my God I made it".

We went out for our first practice. To solidify my spot, I made sure I went out there and caught every ball, ran every route full speed, precise and clean, and made sure that the last few moves didn't include me. I got back to my room after the day, which seemed to be so long with the anticipation, the wondering, the doubt and uncertainty. I told my wife about my day, and she told me to just take the stress off because I put the work in and they won't cut me.

I woke up early the next morning and went in, and the depth charts were on the board. They released their third-round draft pick who was a returner and kept me. When I looked at the depth chart, I was on there for special teams and as a running back. I went from being number 6 on the chart to now being named the starter. I stared at the screen for a good three minutes in shock. I took a picture of the screen, that's how happy I was to see that I had made the team—and not only made it but as the starter. This is too good to be true. This can't be real, am I still dreaming? These were some of the questions I was asking myself.

I know that many of you have been in situations where you've been down and out and had no idea of how you were going to make it. Maybe you are in that situation right now. Things don't stay the same, and you have to demand the change. You can't quit; you can't give up because it didn't happen for you right away. Some things just take time, and in the meantime, just keep working, keep praying, and keep grinding. You will never know how close you are if you give up, that's one thing I learned.

I had finally made a team in the NFL as a starter. I was so used to looking over my shoulder. I expected to make the team, but when it really happened, I was still in awe. Practices were going really well, and my next move was to try to find an apartment. I had to find something that was nice and big enough because I was moving my family down with me. I couldn't keep going on without having them there enjoying the experience with me because I knew I finally would have the money.

I had my first game in a couple days, and I was preparing like I never prepared before. I was really focused and had to make an impact. Now that I had made the team, it was time for me to earn my keep. We flew to Houston, and as close as I was to my family, they couldn't make it down because we didn't plan it right and didn't have the money for gas, hotel stays, and food, so they just stayed at home. We couldn't afford those things because we wouldn't receive our first game check until a few days after the game.

My first regular season game as an NFL player was here, and this one counted. No more pre-season. This was the real deal, and everything counted. We were down the whole first half and were struggling to get anything going on offense. I was having some pretty good kick returns, but we could only manage to get a field goal through the first two quarters. We went in at the half, and the coach was correcting us and getting us adjusted for the next half. I felt like I needed to give us a spark. If I could only see an opening, I would take it all the way back. I had that feeling every time I touched the ball that I could go the distance with a couple key blocks. We came out second half, and we started out on defense. It was a quick three and out, and it was time for the Texans to punt the ball. I remember studying the punter, knowing that he was a left-footed punter, and most of his balls would land to my left. I stood toward the left hash, getting ready to play the ball to my left —but not too far away because he could have gone to my right as well. As I trotted out onto the field, getting my mind right for the return, I put all the pressure on myself, saying I needed to make something happen for my team right now. I looked up as I ran out and thanked God for the opportunity to be out there and also asked to make a difference. I wanted a big return so badly.

The ball was kicked, and as I looked up and saw it falling exactly where I thought it would, I ran over to the spot, looked down the field, and saw the defenders closing in on me. I caught the ball, and there were two guys in my face. I ran to my right, ran right past them, straightened up, and went up the middle of the field. I saw one of my teammates blocking one of the two guys left. I broke past them, and it was myself and the kicker. I put my head down to dig and drive as fast as I could, and I outran the kicker to the touchdown.

At that moment, I knew I had done something a lot of people dreamed of doing, including myself. It happened so fast I didn't know how to react to it, but as always, I dropped to my knee and thanked God and told Crecia that this one was for her. I always said I was going to dedicate my life and all I did to honor her. I felt protected as I was running, and no one could stop me. I was untouched.

That was the first touchdown of the 2012 season for the Dolphins, and I was honored to be the one to do it. After all the letdowns and setbacks, to me, being the first one to score for this NFL team was an amazing turn-around.

As I was running down the field and saw all that space and green grass, I was stunned at how open and how easy that return was. I couldn't believe it happened for me. I always knew I was good enough. I wasn't the number-one draft pick, and I wasn't the most talked about, but I was for sure making a name for myself.

We lost the game, and that sucked because I couldn't enjoy the touch-down as much as I would have if we had won. I was getting a lot of calls from my family and friends, but the person I wanted to see it the most missed it. My wife was with her family and missed the game. To me, it was like a new birth, and I guess it was payback for me. I birthed something new in my life that day, and she missed it. I know she missed a lot of games in Canada and missed a lot of touchdowns I had because our games weren't televised in the United States. It ate me up on the inside, though I know she didn't miss it on purpose; she had four children to try to tend to while going to church and taking care of our home, but it still hurt me. I could only imagine how she felt when I didn't see our children born because I was hurt when she missed my touchdown. Even though she never told me that she was mad or felt some type of way about me not being there, she surely had to.

Sideline Reflections

*"Today I will do what others won't.
So tomorrow I can accomplish what others can't."*

- Jerry Rice.

Consider the story of Jerry Rice.

Rice is widely considered to be the greatest wide receiver in NFL history, and among the greatest NFL players of all time.

He won three Super Bowl rings, and holds over 100 NFL records. Rice was a once-in-a-lifetime talent. Right? Well, not necessarily.

Rice's work ethic and his approach to deliberate practice, are what made him one of the greatest ever. In team workouts, he was famous for his hustle. While many receivers would trot back to the quarterback after catching a pass, Rice would sprint to the end zone after each reception.

He would typically continue practicing long after the rest of the team had gone home.

Most remarkable were his six-days-a-week off-season workouts, which he conducted entirely on his own. These workouts became legendary as the most demanding in the league, and other players would sometimes join Rice just to see what it was like. Some of them got sick before the day was over.

What coach can you hire to help you design the toughest practice routine in your industry?

18
GAME WINNING DRIVE

The hype around our team and what we had going was a little drained after that game. We lost our home opener, but we had some flashes as to we could do. The anticipation of a good season was all that the fans wanted for us. We had the same goal in mind; as we prepared week in and week out, we gave it our all. We were very detailed about our craft but couldn't seem to string together wins. We came home the following week and knew we had to get a win because we were trying to go to the playoffs, and losing wasn't going to get us there.

We had our first home game. I was looking to duplicate what I did in the first game because I'd tasted a little success. I knew we had great game plans in place, and my teammates were selling out when blocking for me because they knew we could be special. We won our next game at home and quieted a lot of the doubt and the critics who were saying we were the same old Dolphins who didn't know how to win. Following that win, we lost two in a row, and things started to heat up around the facility. We knew changes would come if we didn't start winning. Coaches could get fired and players would be cut. The season for me at this point was going well; I was one of the top five kick and punt returners. I was having a lot of success as a returner and started to get reps on offense as I showed the ability to be able to break away. I wanted to get another return so badly. That was the ultimate adrenaline rush for me and one of the fastest ways to turn a game around.

We started getting things on the right track and won two in a row before our bye week. We came off of our bye week and won another game. We finally were putting together some wins. Three in a row, and we felt like we were unstoppable. Our bodies were starting to get a little banged up from the wear and tear of the season, though, and we went on to lose three in a row after just winning three. In the third loss against the Bills, which happened to be a Thursday night game, something special happened. It was my first salute to the troops game, where we supported the armed forces and thanked them for all they did. The Bills' returner, Leodis McKelvin, returned a punt against us, and I was on the sideline, looking and waiting to show them we could do the same thing. Although it'd been a while since I scored a return touchdown, I wanted to respond with one on my own. My teammates walked up to me and challenged me, saying, "Thig, you gon' let him show you up like that?"

I was already thinking I had to get one. I had been getting big returns up until that point, but I hadn't taken it the distance yet. I called the ball at the three-yard line and started up the field. I ran toward the right, but I saw a big hole in their coverage, and instead of following the call we had on, I ran through the hole. It was close to the middle of the field, and when I saw it, I ran as fast as I could through there and saw daylight and the kicker. The kicker came in at me, and I put a few moves on him to where he fell and slid at me, and I jumped over him. I was running and felt someone dive at my feet, and as I was running, I jumped again. I felt someone on the side of me, and I knew I had to outrun him to score because no one else was in front of me. I opened my stride and kept digging and got closer and closer—touchdown Dolphins.

I instantly dropped to my knee and gave praise. I needed this return and hoped there were no holding penalties, as I had a lot of them throughout the year. No flags, and it was indeed a score; we finally got on board. We were down 10-0, and that just gave us a little life. This game was nationally televised and beforehand everyone I knew told me that they would be watching. I can't even begin to explain the emotions that I had going through me. This was something that you had to feel and experience to understand.

As I went back to the sideline, my teammates and coaches were all jumping with me and giving me props. My teammates came up to me and said, "That's how you respond." I was gassed and out of breath from the excitement of the return and had to sit down and control my heart rate before we got back out there. I was still breathing hard the next time out but had to stay composed. We ended up losing the game but as we were headed home, I found out that I was the first player in Dolphins history to return a kick and punt return for touchdowns in the same season. Things were looking good for me up until this point. My numbers were among the best, and I was injury free. I was on a mission to become one of the best returners in the NFL. I had done so from little league, to high school, to college, to the CFL, and now my focus was on the NFL.

The rest of the season was up and down; we won seven games, which wasn't good enough for the playoffs. I was blessed to be on the pro bowl ballot. is was a huge accomplishment for me. I wasn't selected, but to come in as a free agent who didn't get drafted to being on a pro bowl ballot—I was too excited and proud of what I went through to get there. The struggle was beautiful and made things a lot better when the accomplishments started rolling in.

I was doing really well in football, and now things were getting better for me financially. Life was getting easier as the stress was going away regarding how I was going to provide. But while things were going well for me, my family back home was starting to get angry with me because they felt as if I owed them all that I worked hard for. I was doing better but wasn't at a point where I could dish out money. I had four children I was taking care of, bills, and child support, and taxes took half of what I made. Things were easier, but I was not to a point where I could just give out money. When I had to tell my family no, not right now, they thought I was being stingy, but I just didn't have it like that. I ruffled a few feathers and even stopped talking to a lot of family because of money. The one that hurt me the most was my own mother. She and I fell out. I wanted to give my mother the world, but I wasn't in the position to do that yet. I was still trying to take care of old debts and get my crew together, and I couldn't help her out like I wanted. In the meantime, we fell out, and as the word got out about me not helping her, more people started turning their noses up at me.

I was trying to get ready for my second season and capitalize on what I had done in year one, but I couldn't. I couldn't focus like I wanted to because I had people telling me how bad of a person I was when all I was trying to do was help. I sent what I could but it was never enough. It's a lifestyle that some get but others don't, thinking that NFL players make millions of dollars. Some do, but I was the bottom-of-the-barrel player. I was surviving but not thriving like that. I eventually got my family to move down to Florida with me, enrolled our children in school, and was right back in camp. This time it was a little easier, from a family standpoint, because I would have them come see me while I was in the hotel. Any time that we had off, I would drive home to our apartment and spend time there, and that was what I needed. Seeing them refueled me for the next few days I would be away. I wasn't a sure thing with regard to making the team, so I approached this year like I did every other year and made sure I didn't take anything for granted. Even with a good season, I could still be cut at any moment. Nothing is guaranteed in this business, that was my approach. I made sure I kept that same hunger and same fire throughout. I made it through final cuts and was excited to get a new year started. I was more experienced at this level and knew what it took. For our opening game, we were away playing against the Browns.

The punter kicked the ball so high I kind of lost it in the sun. As it was coming down, I found it again, but it was a little too late, and it hit me on my chest (boom). It hit the ground, and I jumped on it and went out of bounds. Flag on the play—it was a penalty against them. I was able to redeem myself right away. I was beating myself up because I had so much space and wanted to open up the season with a touchdown. They backed up five yards and had to re-kick it. The ball was back up high in the air, but this time I knew how to block out the sun and made sure I watched it all the way in. I caught the ball clean, started it up the field, broke to my right, and saw an opening. This can't be that open. Sure enough, it was. I had an entourage of blockers in front of me, knocking people down. I had a guy grab my leg, and I broke out of that tackle. The guys led me into the end zone, and I did my signature kneel down. As I got up and looked back, there was another penalty flag. Come on, please don't be against us. This season couldn't start off any better than this. "Holding" on the return team, touchdown off the board. Back to the sideline again. This time we got the ball way back where I caught it and no touchdown. I was so mad at myself because if I would have caught it the first time, then I wouldn't even be in this position. Those two returns, one good and one bad, wiped each other out. Back to the start for me, and I had to do it all over again. I'm such a perfectionist that I couldn't stop thinking about it.

We went on to win the game but when I don't contribute in a positive way, I don't get too excited. I know we all mess up and make mistakes, but I expect nothing but greatness and couldn't accept any mediocrity.

We won three in a row to start off the season. Things were looking great; we set out to for sure go to the playoffs that year and couldn't let anything hold us back. We had a Monday night game in the Mercedes Benz dome against the Saints, and they were 3-0 as well. Someone was going home with a loss that day and we didn't want it to be us.

We started off doing well and knew we had a chance to win. My most memorable play from this game was a check down pass that I received from Ryan Tannehill. I was our scat back; I went in, faked a block on a blitzing linebacker, and was wide open. Tannehill threw it fast, and I had the safety screaming down to come tackle me. I put a move on him, froze him, and took off. I was so used to being faster than everybody on every level that I played on, and I got too comfortable. I was running down the sideline, looking up at the big screen, knowing I was about to score. I started to slow up as I was about seven yards out, and out of nowhere my heels hit each other, and I was going down face- first into the ground. No, I didn't just get caught, surely no one was behind me. I got up and saw the same guy I had just juked back for revenge. I watched the replay as they showed it up top, and sure enough, his will was greater to stop me than mine was to score, and he got me down on the four-yard line. I was subbed out of the game, and our running back, Lamar Miller, came in and scored the very next play and took my touchdown. I was already in a drought for the year and couldn't get in the endzone. We went on to lose the game. We lost the next four games, and what we thought was a promising year after winning three in a row quickly turned around and went downhill for us. We couldn't get things going at all for a while. But then we put together another three-game winning streak. The last of the three was a game I'll never forget. As a kid, I always had visions of scoring the winning touchdown or scoring the buzzer-beater shot. We were playing the Patriots at home, and we were down three points. It was second and 10 at a minute and twenty seconds left, with playoff hopes alive. My coaches had enough faith in me, a free agent, to put me in to make a play that was designed just for me. I never doubted myself, but the pressure was real. I was one on one of their best linebackers coming out the backfield with a route that I had practiced all year. I beat him with a move and as soon as I turned my head the ball was there. I caught it and ran to the corner of the endzone and knocked the pylon down. Touchdown!!! I ran to the fans, got beer spilled on me and all. We needed a stop, and with Tom Brady in we knew he could drive down and score at will. He drove all the way down and when he threw the last pass up, our safety Michael Thomas got the interception and we won the game. It was just like my last college game when we needed a stop to go to a bowl game

This year things were starting to get better with my relationship with my mom. I wanted my family to see me play, so I flew them down for the game. They didn't see me play in Canada and missed my whole first year. I didn't know if I was blocking my blessings, and I wanted things to get back right, so I made sure to get them down. There I was, a kid from Detroit who had a dream of playing in the NFL, making that dream become a reality. Scoring a touchdown on the game-winning drive started as a dream. What made this even better was knowing that my parents were there to witness it and see me in action. We hadn't beat the Patriots in the last seven games and needed this win to get to the playoffs. We had now won eight games, which was one better than the year before. All we needed to do was win the last two games and we were in there. We had the Jets and the Bills left. We had already beaten the Jets prior and knew we could beat the Bills. But we went out there and lost both the games and threw our amazing season down the drain. We had just beaten the best team in our conference; these games should have been easier for us. We underestimated them and were taken off of our high horse. No playoffs; another promising season down the drain.

End of Third Quarter: Coaching Points

I just try to do the best job I possibly can—put the blinders on, go to work and be the best you can possibly be. Once you have done everything that you possibly can—you've put forth your greatest effort—then I can live with whatever's next.

—Bill Parcels

When it's all said and done, you have to leave no doubt in whatever arena you are in in life. You may put together a great drive and still lose. You may put together a great drive and win. Either way, what you put in is what you get out. If things don't end well, it doesn't necessarily mean you lost. Go back to the drawing board and game plan for the next opponent. Life was never meant to be easy. The hardships we face do nothing but build our character and shape us into who we are today. Let's keep putting together those game-winning drives, one day at a time. Trust the process and don't rush it!

Sideline Reflections

"My great concern is not whether you have failed, but whether you are content with your failure."

- Abraham Lincoln.

My first season with the Miami Dolphins was defined by individual success, but also by some pretty key mistakes. It was also marred by unfortunate strains on some of my personal relationships.

So how does one deal with setbacks that occur despite one's best efforts? Let me give you the example of Abraham Lincoln.

The man who would eventually become the 16th President of the United States, the man who would drive forward the Emancipation Proclamation to free Black slaves, battled crippling depression his entire life.

Known as melancholy, his depression drove him to the brink of suicide twice. He suffered periods of intense brooding, isolation, and pain. His life was defined by enduring and transcending great difficulty.

- Growing up in rural poverty... losing his mother while he was a child.
- Losing the woman he loved to drinking poisonous milk.
- Experiencing multiple defeats at the ballot box, as he made his way through politics.

Lincoln learned to endure and appreciate his difficult conditions. He found purpose in a cause bigger than himself.

If our perspective is limited all we can see is our current situation, then we will never rise beyond our current condition. Lincoln stayed even-keeled with steely determination and will. That allowed him to lead the nation through one of its most difficult and painful periods.

How do you respond to great victories? And how do you respond to devastating losses?

What can you do to ensure that you remain even-keeled through highs and lows?

_____

_____

RESIST & PERSIST

4TH QUARTER

THE DRIVE

19
BACKED UP

The season was over, and my wife and I were making decisions on not paying rent to live anymore. We wanted something in return, and with the season that I had, we started making plans to buy a home. With so much uncertainty, we wanted to make sure we were being smart with our money and investing in the right things. I wanted to make sure that whatever happened with me the following year, we would always have a place to call home. I was being proactive, and we made it happen. My wife found us the best realtors in Texas, Jeffrey and Aricia Blasko. We couldn't make it down to Texas to see homes in person because our children were finishing up the school year. They were kind enough to call us on Skype and take us on virtual tours while we were still in Florida. They were very knowledgeable and taught us everything we needed to know along the way, being first-time homebuyers.

We were on a Skype call, and as they walked into the home to show us the house, we were already sold. We watched as Jeffrey gave us a tour of the home, and we took it off the market that day. We had no idea what it really looked like but we prayed that it was the one for us. We decided that we were going to pack up the car and drive to Texas from Florida to go look at it before we made the final decision. We should have flown but my wife was expecting our third child. She was all for it, so driving it was. The drive was so long; what was supposed to take nineteen hours turned out to be twenty-six. Bathroom breaks, food stops, a couple of rest stops. When we finally made it to Texas and were able to go see our home in person, it took my breath away as I thought back to how things were when I grew up, how we had to stay with family and friends, and moving from apartment to apartment. I snapped back into reality as we walked around, and I was ready to move in right away. I didn't care about any furniture or anything; I wanted to sleep on the carpet in the home. I always had a vision that I would be here, but for it to really happen was unreal. I was smiling like a kid in a candy store.

We went through the process and did all the paperwork, and it was ours. Although we had that long drive back, nothing could take away that feeling I had of being a homeowner. The drive back was a lot easier as I had something to look forward to. A week after I got back from Texas, I went in for practice and was feeling great. I had just put four hundred pounds on the squat rack and did a set of three reps—my new personal best. After our lift, we went outside like we usually did to do our conditioning portion, right before our practice. As usual, I was out there in front of the whole team as we did our sprints. My body was feeling great, I was feeling stronger and faster, and I knew this was about to be a great year. But I had no idea what was coming for me next.

We got done with our run and headed right into position drills. We did a drill where we ran around the garbage can, and as we went around the can, we had to duck under these pipes to simulate staying low, then we had to rise up and catch the ball. As I ducked under, I felt my lower back tightening up. I didn't think anything of it because I had put on a few pounds and felt this pain before, so I was stretching it out so that I could get ready to go run the next drill. I bent over to touch my toes, trying to get my back loosened up, but as I raised up from stretching, the pain didn't leave; and my face told it all. A teammate asked me "Thig, you good?" Not wanting to stop or show any signs of weakness, I told him, "Yeah, I'm straight; my back is just a little tight." I was up next in line to run my route, and as I bent forward to stay low, I fell straight to the ground in pain that I had never experienced before. I had no idea what was going on. This was my first time ever just lying there after being hurt. I never stay down. This can't be happening to me, this is a big year. I don't have time to be hurt. The trainers ran out to get me up as I was looking at the sun shining down on me while sweat rolled down my face. They took me in to run tests and see what was wrong. I was at a point where everything I did hurt me. I couldn't walk, I couldn't stand or sit, and it was even hard to lie down. Anything that I tried was hard for me to do. I was taken to get an MRI. I had a bulging disc in my lower back, and it was hitting a nerve and causing all this pain. This stemmed from a hit that I took the prior year that flared up.

My first thought was that I was done playing football because of the way that I was feeling, and I was nervous because I knew how serious those injuries could be. Dealing with discs, nerves—the only thing that came to my mind was paralysis and the stories I'd seen on it. I didn't know what to expect because I hadn't sustained any serious injuries like this. I'd had injured ankles, shoulders, hamstrings, and wrists, but nothing to this extent.

I was out for a while and couldn't do any football-related activities because I had to allow my back to heal, and although my health was getting better, when playing in the NFL as an undrafted free agent, it's hard to make a team being hurt. Your value decreases tremendously because you're not valuable to the team if you're hurt. The league is a business, and if you don't produce results, then they will move on to someone who is healthy. There are a lot of people trying to take your spot and as mentioned before nothing is guaranteed. Knowing this, I was trying my hardest to get back on the field so that I could compete for a spot on the fifty-three-man roster. One morning before practice, I woke up to several missed calls and text messages from my family. I usually didn't take phone calls during camp because I didn't like to be distracted, but something just didn't feel right.

Sideline Reflections

"Don't fear disaster. Prepare for it. Train for the worst."

- Linda Kaplan Thaler.

There's a fallacy about the power of visualization. Popularized in books like "The Secret," the practice has been largely misunderstood by the general public.

In Linda Kaplan Thaler's book, "Grit to Great: How Perseverance, Passion, and Pluck Take You from Ordinary to Extraordinary," she emphasizes that visualization does have great benefits. But it can actually be harmful when applied the way most of us do it: To the end goal.

Why?

Because fantasizing about achieving the goal (-ex- winning the super bowl) robs us of the motivation to do the hard work required to get there. Our mind gets to experience the feeling of deep satisfaction as if we'd already achieved. And our body, our willpower, our discipline, takes that cue gladly.

If, on the other hand, Kaplan-Thaler posits, we visualize training, deep practice, injuries, and setbacks, we'll actually be able to think through how to handle those potential difficulties.

The right way to do positive thinking: Focus on potential obstacles and how you can overcome them. Don't fear disaster, prepare for it. Train for the worst, and you'll be ready to bounce back.

What are some of the worst-case scenarios that could derail you in the quest for your goal?

And how will you handle those disasters, if they happen?

_____

_____

_____

_____

20
EJECTED

With all that I had going on in my life, I couldn't take on anything else. My load felt heavy, and I had always been the one to carry the team. I had a vision about running track in high school and college and I was always the anchor, last leg on the relay. I often had to either catch people or maintain the lead to get us the win. I had to finish the race, because if I didn't, we would lose. I felt like I was at the tail end of my career due to my back injury, missing practices, and being bumped down on the depth chart. Running the anchor leg so often, I knew what it was like to be last, but because of that, I also knew what it took to beat the odds.

After practice, I called my mom back to see what was going on. My mom told me that my dad was in the hospital because his feet and ankles were swollen. She put him on the phone and, when I talked to him, he seemed upbeat and well. He told me that he had lost a lot of weight since I had seen him last because of some protein deficiency that he had. He then told me that he wanted to come down to Florida with me once he got out so that I could train him, get him bigger and in shape. Of course I was all for it and was honestly shocked he asked me. When we hung up, my pops told me he loved me. I didn't get that often growing up, and I paused and said, "I love you too, Pops; now get out of there and come home."

My pops never really got sick and to me was super healthy. He never went to the doctor because he didn't have insurance and never really needed to. Our relationship was starting to grow and it was about to get better when he came home. A couple days went by, and my pops was still in there, and now I was getting concerned. I asked my mom, "Why is he still there if only his feet and ankles are swollen?" She broke down and told me that it was serious and that I needed to come home ASAP because he wasn't doing well. I said, "Come home? What you mean, he isn't doing well? Where is he?" My back was hurt, and now my dad was sick. I guess when it rains, it pours. I talked my situation over with my coaches and made sure they knew I was leaving. I flew home to see him, and getting on and off the plane was a struggle because my back was hurting so bad. I made it in to see him and when I got there, he was on a breathing machine. What is this? How did all this happen so fast? The doctor explained to me that my dad had a disease called amyloidosis, a form of cancer that attacked all his vital organs. A protein deficiency. He had at most a month to live.

Hearing this news, my heart sank down to my stomach. I was crushed. This can't be happening right now. My dad is so young; he is only forty-four years old and still has to come down and train with me. This can't be it for him, not Pops. I stood there and stared at his lifeless body with all these tubes in his chest, nose, and mouth as the machine did all the breathing for him. I went over and grabbed his hand and said a silent prayer for him as I was rubbing his hand. That back pain that I had seemed like a broken fingernail when I saw the fight that my dad had to go through. The doctor came in and had to move my dad because he couldn't stay in one position too long. As she did that, I wanted to tell her to calm down, be gentle. Did you have to do it that rough? I stayed there for a day, but I had to go back because I had treatments and practice. At this point we had to be in heavy prayer, as his organs had started to shut down one by one.

It was a new season with the new draft class in, and I at least had to give myself a chance. When I finally came back, I felt like I was a step behind. I was rusty; not in the rhythm of doing what I did best, which was to play full speed. I had lost a bit of my conditioning, and playing in that heat made things a lot worse. I was still a bit hesitant because I didn't want to re-aggravate my back. It was better but I still had that tightness.

My pops, back home in Henry Ford Hospital, was in stable condition and was starting to breathe on his own, and his levels were increasing. That news allowed me to worry a little less knowing he was improving. I was at a point where I could play through my pain, but it was still there and I felt it with my every move.

My mom called me and told me my dad had opened his eyes and said a few words. She told him that it was May 21, his only grandson's birthday, and he smiled. She said that while my dad slept, he kept saying "Anchor. . . Markie." My mom didn't know what that meant but knew it had something to do with track, so I told her, "yeah, I used to run the anchor leg." She asked me what that meant—what was he trying to say? I lied and told her that I didn't know, but when I hung up, I told my wife that "anchor leg" meant he was on his last leg.

But with all the good signs he displayed that he would come out on top, he had to, right? He hadn't talked in a week, and now he was talking and his levels were getting back close to normal. The next day, I saw that my mom had called my phone at least fifty times. When someone calls like that, something has to be wrong. I called my mom back to see what was going on. All I heard was crying, gasping for air and pain. I knew at that moment, that was it. My mother said, "Markie, your daddy is gone." I said, "Don't tell me that, Ma. He was just improving; what did the doctors do to him?" I wanted to go home and take my pain and frustration out on the doctors there. I knew that wouldn't get me anywhere, but I was angry, sad, and at a loss for words. I went into my room and cried in disbelief. He had gotten to a point where he had finished the race and was tired of fighting.

One thing that I hate is a funeral, but it was my pops, so I had to be there to pay my respects. I went and saw all my family and friends, and seeing my dad in that casket still hurts me, as I still see visions of him. He was peaceful and looked like he was just taking a nap. My children didn't really understand what was going on and kept asking why I was crying. It seemed like the only reason I was going back to Detroit to visit was to go to a funeral. Still, it was the best feeling to see everyone come together, but not for that reason. The trip was the hardest one I've ever taken, but I'm glad I was able to be there for my mother and siblings. I couldn't stay long and had to get back because of practices and training camp approaching. Going into training camp and pre-season games, I was numb and lost my passion. I knew that things weren't good for me because my playing time was down, and I wasn't producing the way that I knew how.

After losing my dad, my head wasn't in the game anymore. I was ready to hang it up and just be home with my wife and kids. This was my third year with the team, coming from the CFL, having been signed with the Eagles and the Broncos fresh out of college. I was sitting at home when final cuts were being done; this time I didn't have elevators going off to hear people getting their calls. I had my cell phone on me with the ringer on just in case I got the call. I knew I didn't do enough to make the team but I did make some plays; hopefully it was enough.

The day was going by so slowly, and as it got later in the day my phone rang. The call was to come into the coach's office and bring my playbook because the coach wanted to see me. I had been through this process before and knew that there was a possibility of me not making the team. When I went to meet with the coach and the general manager, they started off by saying what a good job I was doing up until that point, and how they respected me and my professionalism. In my mind, I was thinking that they were about to tell me to step my game up because I'd been slacking. They went on to tell me that they didn't feel the need to keep me. I felt a blow to the chest as soon as those words came out. My injury set me back, my pops had passed, and I let those things get to me and stopped fighting. I took a step backward that day, thinking, this year can't get any worse for me. I went back to my apartment where my wife and children were and told Joy the news. She was a bit shocked because I had done so well there, but like always, she kept encouraging me and letting me know that it was another minor setback for a major comeback. I didn't even want to make a comeback; I was down and out.

We now had to move out of the city and go back to our home in Texas that we had recently closed on. Just a day after I got released from the Dolphins, I received a call from the New England Patriots. I thought to myself, what are the odds of me getting a call from the team that I scored the game winning touchdown on and the only game that my pops was able to attend? I was glad that he did get a chance to see me in action once before he left this earth.

Pops,

Thank you for giving me life and always being there for me. I know we didn't get a chance to talk much, but your actions showed me how much you loved me. I promise to be a great father to my children and to keep the legacy going. I'm dedicating the rest of my life to you as you now will live through me. I'm glad you were able to come and see me play in person that one last time. You will never be forgotten. Be ready to work and get swole when I get there.

I love you.

Your oldest son,

"Marky Mark"

Sideline Reflections

"The LORD is near to the brokenhearted.
And saves the crushed in spirit."

- Psalms 34:18.

Sometimes, when it rains, it pours.

Throughout my life, I've learned that we can turn trial into triumph, if we practice:

1. Choosing the right perspective

2. Taking the right action, and

3. Building our internal will power.

That willpower is what I had to bring to bear this chapter of my life. Will is our internal power, which can never be affected by the outside world.

It is our final trump card.

If action is what we do when we still have some ability to affect the situation, then WILL is what we depend on when that ability has all but disappeared.

The loss of my father just about sapped every last ounce of will I had, but I held on.

What are you relying on to get you through?

_____

21
A NUMBERS GAME

By this time, I'd been cut four times, and it was starting to get to me. One thing that was common with all the cuts was that I was always told it was a numbers game. I never really understood that until the cuts kept happening and the jersey kept changing. I was always trying to figure out why whatever jersey number I wore on a particular team couldn't be a part of the numbers that were spared. In Philly, I wore number 13, in Denver, I wore number 38, in Saskatchewan, I wore number 38 again, in Hamilton, I wore number 8, and in Miami, I was now saying good-bye to number 34. In my fifth season of professional football, I had been a part of five different teams, wore five different jerseys, and was expecting my another child. But I was still determined to make my Crecia and my dad proud, regardless of the number I wore.

- Patriots #33: My agent told me that the Patriots wanted me to come in to be on the practice roster. I told my agent I'd think about it. I was a starter for the last five years, and they wanted me to be a practice player. I just scored a game-winning touchdown on them the previous year—I know they remembered. This call reminded me of when I was called into the office at Indiana University and the coach told me I was being redshirted to develop. I didn't want to accept the offer because I felt I was worth more than that. I had just been playing, I had success, I held records. I guess that didn't count.

After talking with my wife and agent and listening to them tell me to keep pursuing my dream, I accepted the offer, and they flew me out that same day. In the meantime, I had to fly my sister-in-law, and two of my close friends, Kevin and Savage, in to help Joy pack up our apartment in the U-Haul and drive it twenty hours to our home in Texas. I got my truck shipped down to where I was in Foxborough while they drove the U-Haul and my wife's truck to Texas. I have a great group of friends and I could have called any of them, but these two came without hesitation. I'm a firm believer that everything happens for a reason, and I say this because we had decided to buy a home prior to all of this. Not knowing that this would happen five months later, it was one of the best decisions that we made. Our plan from that point was to get my wife and kids back to Texas as soon as possible; she was already eight months pregnant and needed to get somewhere stable fast while I figured out what was next for me.

When I got to New England, I was already behind because they had a whole off-season and training camp together, and I didn't know anything. I was starting all the way over with a new team, new coaches, new plays, and everything was foreign to me. I had in my mind that I would be there for that year at least because I played and started, so I should for sure be good enough for the practice roster. Practice was going well; I was learning the playbook and my new teammates, and things were going smoothly. After a week and a half, I went out and got an apartment with a former teammate who played in Miami with me.

The very next day after signing the lease, I got the call again and was told that they needed my roster spot to make room on their roster for some defensive guy to come in. They told me that they were going to keep me in mind for sure because they liked what they saw. I went back to the apartment that I'd just signed the lease for and laid down on my air mattress. That same day, I decided to pack my truck up and hit the road. At this point, I just wanted to go home and call it quits for the year. I told a couple of the guys who were over that I was leaving and driving home to Texas. They thought I was playing around but I already had my mind made up. I knew I had a twenty-seven-hour drive ahead of me. I had been released from two teams in less than a month and was ready to go home and re-evaluate some things.

In football, a player who is late for a meeting, misses a practice, or even wears the wrong color of shoes can be fined. I was on time and did everything right but I felt like I was being fined, and they were taking money out of my family mouth. Maybe it was really time for me to hang it up. I had a successful career and played at the highest level possible and did well. I broke a record in Miami, being the first player to score a kick return touchdown and a punt return touchdown in the same season. I was also ranked in the top five in both categories. These were some of the thoughts in my head as I was driving, thinking about what I would do next. I was always told that NFL stood for Not for Long, and I was noticing that. On my way home my agent, Rob Sheets, gave me a call and told me that the Indianapolis Colts wanted to bring me in for a workout after I made it home to Texas. I made one stop on the whole drive back to Texas, and that was a rest stop for an hour to take a nap. Other than that I only stopped to get gas and food. I did a lot of praying and sightseeing along the way, listening to my Eric Thomas mixtapes, church sermons, and my old-school R&B. I finally made it home and was so happy to get there. Seeing my beautiful wife and kids' faces made everything so much better for me.

- Dolphins #19: I was home for three days after my workout with the Colts before my agent gave me another call and told me that the Miami Dolphins, my original team, wanted to bring me back in to be on their practice squad. I was surprised and confused at the same time. I was just released from there, and now they wanted me back? I wasn't sure why. I'm the type of person who never quits or gives up, but I was getting weak. People only see the bright side of things when it comes to playing professional sports. There is a downside and I was in it.

What I want people to realize is that there are a lot of sacrifices that you have to make to live your dream. It's what we signed up for but it doesn't make it any easier. Chasing my dream, I missed all of my children's births, except for one. I missed first steps, potty training, school plays, graduations, and first football games. I missed first cheerleading competitions and practices, and that's time that I will never get back. When I started putting things into perspective, I would sit back and ask myself, is all this even worth it? Finances were better than they'd ever been. But... was it worth the cost of missing time that I would never get back? There is no rewind button. Pictures and videos make things easier but not being there really affects the children as well as me.

I did accept the offer and went back, and honestly it felt great to be back around familiar faces and back where it started for me. It was in the midst of the season, and while I was back in Miami, my wife and children stayed at home in Texas; she could go into labor at any moment. I got the call one day that it was time, and I went straight to Philbin the head man and let him know that I was leaving to go home. I didn't know what we were having, a boy or girl, because we wanted to be surprised at birth as to what the gender was.

My wife's sister sent me a picture from the operating room of my daughter, Morgyn, as she was born on October 9, 2014. Once again, I missed another birth but I was there to hold her moments afterward.

I stayed home for only two days before I had to get back to practice. A week later, I was released, and I don't know if it had anything to do with me going home but, once again, I was out of a job. I was really starting to get fed up with playing ball because things just weren't working out the way I planned. This wasn't only affecting me but also my wife, and now my kids were starting to ask why I kept switching teams. I'd try to explain to them the reasons behind it but it was taking a toll on all of us. My five-year-old son said to me, "Daddy, I want you to come home." That brought tears to my eyes to hear him say that. It really penetrated my heart to know that he really understood that Daddy wasn't there, and he needed me. I was already preparing my mind and heart to transition to a new job. I was home another week before another call came in.

- Buccaneers #19: This call was from the Tampa Bay Buccaneers. I talked to my wife and friends, and like every other time, they all wanted me to go and do the workout and show the league what they were missing out on. I flew there and checked into the hotel they had set up for me. Just like the Colts, they put me through a physical the following morning before we got started. They had brought in another returner and myself, and they were going to sign one of us for sure that day. I had a great workout and was called into the office, where I was told that they were going to keep the other returner but they really wanted to keep us both. I was told to fill out a form, which had where I wanted to fly to after leaving there. As soon as I got done with the form, I was called back in the office. The head scout told me, "We found a way to keep you both, and since you still have practice squad eligibility, we want to keep you on the practice squad." He went on to say, "You never know what may happen; injuries do occur, so don't get complacent there." Sure enough, I was on the practice roster for two weeks before the other returner, Trindon Holiday, got hurt.

In this league you have to stay healthy to stay on a team. I was finally moved back up to the active roster, and I thought to myself that this was all worth it. I had been cut time and time again; this was now my seventh pro team. I was grinding so hard and putting in so many hours. I read some books and heard a lot of successful people say that to be successful and world-class, you have to put in ten thousand hours. I've spent count-less hours praying and reading. I knew my best days were ahead of me.

Through the whole journey, my faith never wavered.

I played in four games; three of them were good. I had a game where I made a terrible decision on a punt by letting it hit the ground and then tried to pick it up, and by me touching the ball, it was considered a muff and the other team recovered it. The rest of the game was good, with good decisions, but we were having a bad season, and there was zero tolerance there. I was called back in the office. I was told, "You're a great player, we love everything about you, but we just can't have turnovers, so we are going to go in a different direction. We know you are good enough to play in this league but we are in a bind right now and have to let you go." I was for sure done now and ready to shut it down.

They flew me home, and it was two days before Thanksgiving. Everyone was happy to see me; there is no greater feeling than to come home and have my crew run up to me and give me hugs and kisses. They had goody bags and signs for me that said, "Welcome home, Daddy," with pictures that they drew. Things like that made the pain go away. My wife asked me how I felt about everything and what I wanted to do. I told her, "Whatever happens next, just know that I will be here for Thanksgiving to celebrate it in our new home. Nothing or no one was going to change that." I told her and my friends that I was done for the year, and I was going to train, get back 100% healthy, and try again next year.

My personal plans weren't in alignment with God's plans, though, and He surely has a sense of humor because as soon as I got home, I was getting calls and emails and texts.

- Bills #11: Rob was blowing my phone up, call after call, text after text. He was even calling my wife's phone. I ignored every call that came to my phone. I had an unknown number calling me as well, and I didn't know who was calling or why. What I did know was that I wasn't going anywhere; I was staying home. I was on this crazy journey, and I just wanted to sit down, spend some family time and clear my mind. My wife and I talked every day and always wondered why we had to go through this. We were always apart and really couldn't enjoy our union like we both hoped we could. I was being tested left and right and didn't know why. There was so much happening, so much uncertainty, and all I could do was lean on my family and friends for comfort as I was going through this season of my life.

The same number kept calling, and I kept ignoring it. Finally, I got a text that said, "Marcus, we have claimed you off waivers," which means that when you get released from a team, there's a twenty-four-hour grace period where a team can pick up your previous contract. The text went on to say, "We are about to send you your flight information." I was thinking to myself, who is this? I was unpacking and hanging all my clothes up in my closet and was determined to take a stand until I saw that text.

An email followed with my flight itinerary, along with another text from my agent yelling at me through the text, saying I was about to miss this opportunity. I finally responded and called back to see who it was, and it was the Buffalo Bills.

There's a rule that when you're claimed off waivers, you have to be active for four games. Knowing that, I knew I had an opportunity to go right in and play in four games. Their returner got hurt, and they wanted to bring me in to fill that void. Everything was already moving so fast, and this just added to it. I got to Buffalo on Thanksgiving morning at 2:00 a.m. and had practice that day. All of my teammates and coaches were so welcoming and made me feel like I was wanted. It was a feeling that I hadn't had with any other team. I was fortunate enough to have a friend and old teammate from the CFL named Jeremy Kelley who lived in Buffalo. I was invited over to his home to have a nice home-cooked Thanksgiving meal. I practiced that day, and we got off early because of the holiday. We had one more practice that Friday. We had a walk-through Saturday, and I was dressed, active, and playing that Sunday. Returning isn't too bad to come in and play because you can really only go left, right, or middle. That's everywhere you go, and every return is different due to schemes but a lot of them are similar.

I had a great first game. After praying and asking God why and what all this was for, I knew it was meant for me to be there. The next week, we played against, arguably, the best team in the league that year, the Green Bay Packers. We were down 3-0 in the first quarter, and our defense had just gotten a huge third-down stop. It was a very windy day and they came out to punt the ball. They had one of the best coverage units in the league for the last four years and hadn't allowed a return for a touchdown against them since 2011. I knew that going in because of film study and looking at their stats. They were stout and really didn't have any weaknesses.

The ball was punted, and the wind caught it, and it hung in the air for a bit. I ran up under it and caught it in front of one of my teammates Marquise Gray who was supposed to be blocking for me. It fell so short that he even dropped back too deep. After I caught it, there were four guys in my face, but no one to my left. I shot to my left, and it was wide open. I was striding down the field with two blockers in front of me, Bacarri Rambo and Nikel Roby, and they led me downfield. I cut back to my right and had to stiff-arm a player, and the kicker and got tripped up and flipped into the end zone. I gave the ball away to a fan, dropped to my knee, and told my pops that was for him. I scored the only touchdown for our team, and it was on that seventy-five-yard punt return. I was so excited, and after all that I had gone through over the course of the year, it was all worth it. I began to regain sight of where I once had been. I knew I had it in me, I just needed another opportunity. I was honored when I was able to share that moment with the team.

We won that game and gave ourselves a chance to be in the playoffs. We needed to win the last two games to go to the playoffs. We went out to Oakland, knowing we were going to win, and lost.

No playoffs, even though we were 9-7, which was the best record I had been a part of.

I had signed a two-year contract and knew I was coming back next season, but like every other contract, nothing is guaranteed. I came home after the whirlwind of a year that I had and just sat down for two weeks. I was still working out but other than that, I didn't want to do anything but relax. I was on the road and went from team to team, and now I'd finally found a home. I came into camp the following year in great shape. I won our off-season "Iron Man" trophy as I outworked the rest of the team. I was physically and mentally prepared. That camp was one of the best camps I've had. Rex Ryan came in and brought a lot of excitement with him. He is the definition of a true player's coach, and he made sure he took care of our bodies during camp. I took a hit on my lower back in one of our practices, and my back flared up again. It wasn't as bad as it was before, but it was pretty close. I missed a few days due to my injury but was still able to move around. I knew what happened last time I was in that position, and I wasn't going to let it happen again. I got back out there and fought through the pain and tried making plays every day.

Soon, I was back to the position of final cuts and awaiting the "call process." The day went by, and I didn't get a call, which was great news. I went in to practice the next day as we started to get ready for the opener and saw a lot of guys gone. We had to cut the roster down from ninety to fifty-three, which means we were thirty-seven guys shorter.

My wife and I had no idea what was going to happen with me but we knew we wanted to be together. We made the decision to homeschool our children so they could travel and be with me on the road. The burden of that fell on my wife, mostly, but I would come to our hotel room after practice and would help out as much as I could.

The season started off kind of shaky with a win, loss, win, loss. I hadn't scored any touchdowns, but I did have some pretty good returns and worked in on offense. One day, I was going about business as usual and went in for breakfast before meetings, and our scouting director asked to see me. I went with him and met with the head of the scouting department. He told me that they were going to release me because they were looking for a spark on special teams. I guess I wasn't doing enough. This came as a complete surprise for me; I did not see that coming. I went back to the room and shared the news with my family, and they were mad. We packed up all that we had, packed up the truck, and drove back to Texas once again. When we made it home, I told my wife that I was for sure done. I was just talking before, but I was getting serious about calling it quits. The only thing that stopped me from quitting was that I wasn't a quitter. I was home for a week before I got a call.

- Colts #14: The Colts called me and wanted to sign me right away because they were looking for a spark on their special teams. They had worked me out prior and expressed interest, and they held their end of the bargain by bringing me in. I flew there, signed the contract, and got right back to work. Things were looking good, and I was about to play my first game with the hometown team of the college I went to. I was excited to be back where it all started for me. This was a top-of-the-line organization, and they were very thorough. Training staff and coaches were top-of-the-line. Practices were going really well, and I was picking up the playbook pretty well here as well. The day before the game, I got yet another call, and all the preparation and everything I put into that week went out the window. They cut me because of an injury, and they needed my roster spot. At this point, I was at the bottom of the barrel, being bounced around and around. I flew home once again; it was back to the drawing board. I was home for a week, and then another call came in. I can honestly say that I am so grateful for all of these opportunities but I don't think my heart can take any more of this.

- Raiders #19: I didn't want to keep bouncing around but I couldn't give up yet. I wanted to keep going until I was told no. The Raiders flew me out and signed me right away. They had a guy get injured as well, and I was there to fill his spot. I played in the first game against the Steelers and only had one return that game because our defense couldn't get them off the field. They covered it pretty well and held me to a short gain.

My experience here was pretty good. The weather was always nice, but the locker room looked like a high-school locker room. The weight room was top-of-the-line and by far the best one I've ever seen. The next game was approaching, and we were about to play at home. I had played here previously, but I was on the opposing team. The day before the game, it happened again. I got the call to come into the office, and sure enough, I was being released again. I kept failing, kept being let down, but I knew the plan had to be greater than this. I'd been down before, but after being knocked down so much, it takes a toll on a person. I could have given up a while ago, but I pressed on.

I went home and didn't hear anything for a couple weeks. It was close to Thanksgiving time again, and there were no calls. I was happy about it because I hadn't had a chance to spend a holiday in my home since we bought it. It was time. We had the menu together, we invited friends and family, and I was excited to be around everyone. As we were grocery shopping to get the food, my phone rang.

- Bills #11: My agent was on the phone, telling me that the Buffalo Bills wanted to bring me in for a workout. I said, "For a workout? Workout for what? They know what I can do. They saw me play already, and I know the plays still." He told me that they were going to pick between me and another returner for the job after the workout. I was fed up with it all and told him, "I'm not doing another workout, especially for a team that I once played for." I said, "It's two days before I get to spend Thanksgiving at home. The other guy can have the job."

He called and told them what I said, and I guess it all made sense to them, so they said, "OK, give us a little time, and we will call back." They called back and said, "We aren't going to work the other guy out, we are just going to sign you. How soon can you get to the airport?" They flew me out that same day, and there I was, a whole year later, back with the same team a day before Thanksgiving—the same time I came the prior year. I was spending Thanksgiving alone yet again.

One of my good friends, my teammate, Marquise Goodwin, saw me at the airport shortly after I told him the news as I was flying back to Buffalo. He asked where I was staying when I got back, and I told him I was going back to the Staybridge Suites, where I had stayed prior. I'd learned to not sign another lease because I knew nothing was guaranteed, and I didn't want to break another one. Without hesitation, he offered me his spot until the end of the year because he wasn't going to be there; he was on injured reserve and was done for the year. I took him up on that offer and soon after I arrived, I made sure to get my family on a flight to come back down.

When I got there, all of the guys were happy to see me, and I had that same welcoming that I'd had the first time I was there. The fans even showed me love. I felt right back at home again, and I didn't get that feeling anywhere else.

It was back to business as usual, and things were going well. My back started acting up again, but I was at a point where I could battle through it now. Everything was going smoothly. Then we played the Eagles at their home, and I took a chance and tried to catch a punt while a guy was in my face. I muffed it, and they recovered it. That was it; my heart dropped, and I was pissed at myself. Why didn't I just fair-catch it? I was out there trying to do too much; I was too anxious to get a score and it hurt the team. I put that loss on my back and took it to heart because I could have possibly blown our playoff chances. I knew I was for sure getting cut after that. We got back, and every day I was waiting for someone to come get me and tell me that I was done there. It didn't happen, and I kept going. We played the Redskins in a must-win game, and we lost it. We were down to our last two games.

It was two days before Christmas when the scout I was waiting on came and got me. He told me that they wanted to try out their rookies who were on the practice squad to see what they had. He apologized that it happened the way it did, two days before Christmas. Although he apologized, it didn't make anything better and I was done for sure at this point.

When I think of Persisting through Resistance I can't help but to think of myself. I consider my life - the ups, the downs, the twists, the turns and I think of the possibilities. Walking away from the scene of that accident all those years ago, who would've thought that I'd even have the opportunity to make it as far as I have in my career? The trauma alone of losing someone you love, in the way that it happened, is enough for anyone to give up, "check out" on life. Combine that with the, seemingly, never ending saga of rejection after rejection after rejection, and I have to tell you, if it wasn't for God giving me the will, fight, and determination to keep going in spite of the circumstances, I don't know where I would be today.

Fact is, you don't get to choose the hand you're dealt. Life is a matrix of decisions and the consequences of those decisions. If you're lucky, you may get a few breaks here and there, but for the most part, you are what you've chosen to be. Some may look at my journey and call it any number of things, but they can never say that I wasn't committed, that I wasn't resilient, or that I wasn't sincere. Resistance is subjective in nature but the mindset needed to persevere past it isn't. No, you don't get to choose the hand you're dealt, but with the right attitude, you can walk away from the table victorious. It's a decision made only by you.

Sideline Reflections

What does Persevering beyond the Limitations of life mean to you?

_____

_____

What commitments can you make to yourself moving forward to make sure that you are putting forth your best foot, best effort despite opposing circumstances?

Dear Fans,

My journey was hard—long days and nights. A lot of blood, sweat, and tears. It was a lot of ups and downs and smiles and frowns. I had some great times and terrible times. Through it all, I want to thank you for the support that you have given me through the years. The ride and the journey was fun, and I'm extremely blessed to say I played with and against some of the best. I don't know what's next for me, but I will always give whatever I do 120%. I've never been the one to quit, but I've prayed and talked about what I want to do next. All good things must come to an end. I don't know what my future holds but I will be prepared to take on whatever life throws at me.

God Bless.

Yours truly,

THIGGY

Eric Thomas: Words can't explain the things that you brought out of me. You taught me how to fight, how to never give up, to always give it my all. Your growing up and making it out of the same city, same high school I started out at, gave me hope. Being ministered to through your videos and having an opportunity to meet you was a tremendous blessing. I learned to use my pain for a greater purpose beyond myself. Thank you for all the support, for the belief in me, and, most importantly, the relationship we have. One thing that will always stick with me is to never let my current circumstance dictate my future opportunities.

www.ingramcontent.com/pod-product-compliance
Lightning Source LLC
Chambersburg PA
CBHW051405070526
44584CB00023B/3294